VMware Horizon Workspace Essentials

Manage and deliver a secure, unified workspace
to embrace any time, any place, anywhere access to
corporate apps, data, and virtual desktops securely
from any device

Peter von Oven

Peter Björk

Joel Lindberg

BIRMINGHAM - MUMBAI

VMware Horizon Workspace Essentials

Copyright © 2014 Packt Publishing

First published: March 2014

Production Reference: 1130314

Published by Packt Publishing Ltd.
Livery Place
35 Livery Street
Birmingham B3 2PB, UK.

ISBN 978-1-78217-237-6

www.packtpub.com

Cover Image by Tony Shi (shihe99@hotmail.com)

Credits

Authors

Peter von Oven

Peter Björk

Joel Lindberg

Reviewers

Andrew Alloway

Luigi Danakos

Joe Jessen

Ryan Johnson

Lauren Malhoit

Mario Russo

Maarten Vekens

Acquisition Editor

Mohammad Rizvi

Content Development Editor

Mohammed Fahad

Technical Editors

Adrian Raposo

Sebastian Rodrigues

Copy Editors

Roshni Banerjee

Janbal Dharmaraj

Deepa Nambiar

Karuna Narayanan

Project Coordinator

Sanket Deshmukh

Proofreader

Maria Gould

Indexer

Hemangini Bari

Production Coordinator

Arvindkumar Gupta

Cover Work

Arvindkumar Gupta

About the Authors

Peter von Oven is an experienced technical consultant and has spent the last 20 years of his IT career working with customers and partners in designing technology solutions aimed at delivering true business value. During his career, Peter has been involved in numerous large-scale enterprise projects and deployments, presented at key IT events, and has worked in senior pre-sales roles for some of the giants of IT. Over the last eight years, Peter has focused his skills and experience within the end user computing market, and today he leads the End User Computing Pre Sales team at VMware in the UK&I, tasked with delivering the next generation of end-user computing and workforce mobility solutions.

Peter got his first taste for writing last year while assisting with some of the chapters in the book *Building End-User Computing Solutions with VMware View, Lulu,* and got the writing bug. He went on to write his own book, *VMware Horizon Mirage Essentials, Packt Publishing,* which was published in December 2013.

> I would like to thank my wife and my two daughters for their continued support while I have spent many an evening and weekend at the keyboard. Finally, I would also like to thank my co-authors, Peter Björk and Joel Lindberg. It's been great sharing ideas and collaborating during the writing of this book.

Peter Björk has many years' experience in VMware Horizon Workspace and ThinApp. He started out working with Thinstall, and continued after VMware acquired the product in 2008, renaming it ThinApp. Peter supports Horizon Workspace and ThinApp in the Europe, Middle East, and Africa region. As a teacher, Peter has educated many ThinApp packagers around the world. Peter lives in Sweden with his wife and two kids, a boy and a girl. Peter Björk is very active on the VMware community pages and the official VMware Workspace and ThinApp blogs. You can follow Peter on Twitter (@thepeb) to get the latest ThinApp and Workspace news.

Peter Björk published his first book, *VMware ThinApp 4.7 Essentials*, *Packt Publishing*, in 2012.

I would like to thank the people who have supported me throughout the writing of this book. First and foremost, my thanks go out to my wonderful wife, Lena. Many thanks to my two wonderful kids, Albin and Filippa, who constantly remind me of what's important in my life. Many thanks to my co-writers, Joel Lindberg and Peter von Oven; it has been a pleasure working with you.

Joel Lindberg has 20 years' experience in the IT industry in various positions and is currently working at VMware as a Senior Systems Engineer specializing in end-user computing solutions. He has spoken at VMworld several times and is an active member and moderator on the VMware user communities. Joel interacts with customers, partners, and vendors, and has been involved in many successful customer projects. You can follow him on Twitter (@viewgeek).

Joel lives in Stockholm, Sweden with his family.

I would like to thank my wife for supporting me in writing this book and my co-authors Peter Björk and Peter von Oven for their guidance and good judgment.

About the Reviewers

Andrew Alloway was born and raised in Edmonton, Canada. He graduated from the University of Alberta with a Computer Science degree.

Working at Nuna Logistics Limited, he supported northern mining sites in its unique and challenging IT environment. In 2012, some of his projects and work was featured in the Winter 2012 edition of Aptitude Magazine in an article entitled *Building the road to streamlined license agreements*.

He is a supporter of open source technology and products including Ubuntu, ICTFax, Apache, Drupal, Piler, and various other projects.

He has designed and implemented projects including Exchange migrations, Lync deployments, System Center Configuration Manager, and various other VMware products.

In 2013, Andrew attained his VMware Certified Professional 5 Data Center Virtualization certification.

I would like to thank my family for all the support I have received over the years, and my employers for investing in the development of my skills and career.

Luigi Danakos has been in the technology industry for 11 years. He likes helping people understand technology. He is currently the CEO for Blurt Media Group, a technical and social media consultation firm. When not playing with technology, Luigi enjoys spending his time with his family, inspiring his kids to do what they love, by doing what he loves.

I would like to thank my family for their love and support in all my endeavors. They are the real inspiration behind all that I do. Honorable mention should go out to the #NerdHerd for always being there for each other to listen and vent when needed.

Joe Jessen currently works at Dell, but as a veteran in the IT industry, has held roles in private corporations, technology vendors, and consulting organizations. Joe has been involved with application and desktop delivery since 1996, setting the strategic direction for global organizations with their end user computing initiatives. With a focus on virtualization, Joe has also been an Industry Analyst in the end user computing and desktop virtualization space for The Virtualization Practice (www.virtualizationpractice.com) and Solutions 101, LLC (www.solutions101.us). Joe was also a technical reviewer for the book *VMware Horizon View 5.3 Design Patterns and Best Practices, Packt Publishing*. You can follow him on Twitter @JoeJessen or connect with him on LinkedIn at http://www.linkedin.com/pub/joe-jessen/0/666/336/.

Ryan Johnson is a staff technical account manager working for VMware as a part of Professional Services. He has over 18 years of enterprise experience ranging from engineering, research and development, enterprise technology and business architecture, service management, and professional services.

Prior to joining VMware, he was the Enterprise Technology Architect for Citizens Property Insurance Corporation of Florida where he led the enterprise architecture program and was responsible for the aspects of technology, applications, and information architecture.

He holds numerous industry certifications from VMware, Microsoft, EMC, Red Hat, and others.

For a mix of hypertext fragments, pixels, and all things under-analyzed, follow him on Twitter @tenthirtyam or on LinkedIn (linkedin.com/in/tenthirtyam).

Lauren Malhoit has been in the IT field for over 10 years and has acquired several data center certifications. She's currently a technical virtualization architect specializing in virtualization and storage in the data center. She has been writing for a few years for TechRepublic, TechRepublic Pro, and VirtualizationSoftware. com. As a Cisco Champion, EMC Elect, VMware vExpert, and PernixPro, Lauren stays involved in the community. She also hosts a bi-weekly technology podcast called AdaptingIT (http://www.adaptingit.com/). Lauren has been a delegate for Tech Field Day several times as well. She has authored *vCenter Operations Manager Essentials, Packt Publishing*, and was also a technical reviewer for *OpenStack Cloud Computing Cookbook - Second Edition, Packt Publishing*.

Mario Russo has worked as an IT Architect, a Senior Technical VMware Trainer, and in the pre-sales department. He has also worked on VMware Technology since 2004.

In 2005, he worked for IBM on the First Large Project Consolidation for Telecom Italia on the Virtual VMware Esx 2.5.1 platform in Italy with the Physical to Virtual (P2V) tool.

In 2007, he conducted a drafting course and training for BancoPosta, Italy, and project disaster and recovery (DR Open) for IBM and EMC.

In 2008, he worked for the Project Speed Up Consolidation BNP and the migration P2V on VI3 infrastructure at BNP Cardif Insurance.

He is a VCI Certified Instructor 2s Level of VMware and is certified in VCAP5-DCA.

He is the owner of Business to Virtual, which specializes in virtualization solutions.

He was also the technical reviewer of the books *Implementing VMware Horizon View 5.2*, *Implementing VMware vCenter Server*, *Troubleshooting vSphere Storage*, and *VMware Horizon View 5.3 Design Patterns and Best Practices*, all by *Packt Publishing*.

I would like to thank my wife Lina and my daughter Gaia. They're my strength.

Maarten Vekens is a 33 year old freelance system administrator. He is certified in VMware Certified Associate and Data Center Virtualization. He is currently living in Brussels, Belgium.

He is an amateur cyclist who travels around the world and enjoys the cultural life.

He started his IT career 15 years ago at one of the biggest Petrochemical companies in the world. After some other project, he was asked to join the IT staff at Belga News Agency. While on this project, he started to work with VMware.

In 2012, he started his own company, Takeitoff (www.takeitoff.be), together with his best friend Vincent Oomen. They offer services to the European Commission and the Thomas Cook Airlines. The main focus stays on system administration and program management.

www.PacktPub.com

Support files, eBooks, discount offers and more

You might want to visit www.PacktPub.com for support files and downloads related to your book.

Did you know that Packt offers eBook versions of every book published, with PDF and ePub files available? You can upgrade to the eBook version at www.PacktPub.com and as a print book customer, you are entitled to a discount on the eBook copy. Get in touch with us at service@packtpub.com for more details.

At www.PacktPub.com, you can also read a collection of free technical articles, sign up for a range of free newsletters and receive exclusive discounts and offers on Packt books and eBooks.

http://PacktLib.PacktPub.com

Do you need instant solutions to your IT questions? PacktLib is Packt's online digital book library. Here, you can access, read and search across Packt's entire library of books.

Why Subscribe?

- Fully searchable across every book published by Packt
- Copy and paste, print and bookmark content
- On demand and accessible via web browser

Free Access for Packt account holders

If you have an account with Packt at www.PacktPub.com, you can use this to access PacktLib today and view nine entirely free books. Simply use your login credentials for immediate access.

Instant Updates on New Packt Books

Get notified! Find out when new books are published by following @PacktEnterprise on Twitter, or the *Packt Enterprise* Facebook page.

Table of Contents

Preface

In the last few years, the market has exploded with new devices, applications, and services that have been focused on being easy to access and consumable with little technical knowledge. It's pretty much now become the norm to visit an online store, choose an application, and start using it immediately.

The traditional approach has been to deploy Windows on physical machines and use some form of distribution system for deploying applications and securing data. Users would be working from 9 to 5 in the office, physically sitting in front of their desktop PCs, and therefore they would consider it secure.

Corporate IT risks turning into a slow-moving dinosaur that does not contribute, but rather hinders innovation and the users' ability to be productive. Users are starting to avoid involving IT since it takes a long time to get anything done, and is slow moving. There is now a real threat that corporate IT becomes irrelevant and starts getting competition from these outside trends.

VMware has a track record in innovation, often where others get stuck. The origin of Horizon Workspace was a cloud identity services platform called MyOneLogin. It was developed by a company called TriCipher. TriCipher was founded in 2000 and acquired by VMware in August 2010.

Horizon Application Manager 1.0 was released in May 2011. This was also the first time that VMware unveiled their Project Horizon vision, with Application Manager being the first solution delivered against that vision. Horizon Application Manager was a user-centric management service for accessing cloud applications and included an identity-as-a-service hub that securely extended the users' existing identity, and allowed users to access web-based applications in a secure manner from any device.

Since the solution was still a cloud service, one of the top priorities for VMware was to convert it into an on-premise solution. (This was highly in demand especially by European customers who have strict data privacy laws.)

In August 2011, VMware released Horizon Workspace 1.5, and now customers could choose to install it on premise. During 2011, VMware acquired other companies such as Wanova to expand their capabilities. Horizon Suite 1.0 was announced in the spring of 2013. The idea with the Suite is that the customer could now buy one **Stock Keeping Unit (SKU)** to solve all their needs for end-user computing, from managing physical desktops to mobile management. The Suite includes Horizon Workspace, Horizon View, and Horizon Mirage, along with ThinApp, Workstation, and Fusion.

What this book covers

Chapter 1, Getting Started with VMware Horizon Workspace, gives you an overview of all the components you need to have in place before you start the installation process of Horizon Workspace.

Chapter 2, Design, Install, and Configure, covers the basic sizing, configuration, and the installation of Horizon Workspace 1.5. After making sure that all the prerequisites are in place, we will start deploying Horizon Workspace.

Chapter 3, Horizon Files, looks at the architecture behind Horizon Files and then enables and configures this feature.

Chapter 4, Integrating SaaS Applications, covers one of the core features of Horizon Workspace, that is the ability to entitle and consume web-based applications. In this chapter, we will talk about SAML authentication and how to configure Horizon Workspace to broker to SaaS applications.

Chapter 5, Mobile Management, discusses the mobile management capabilities of VMware Horizon Workspace 1.5, including configuration, device enrollment, and how to entitle users to mobile applications.

Chapter 6, Integrating ThinApp Packages, will look at how to manage Windows-based applications using VMware ThinApp.

Chapter 7, Horizon View Integration, will talk about how to integrate Horizon View so that the users can access their virtual desktop directly from their Workspace.

Chapter 8, Troubleshooting, will cover the most common issues that come up during the installation and configuration of Horizon Workspace.

Appendix, Useful Links, provides a number of useful links for additional information and references used in this book.

What you need for this book

To get the most out of this book, you should have some experience of working as an IT administrator with skills and knowledge on building and designing end user environments, and have an understanding of the challenges faced by users.

Throughout the book, you have the opportunity to follow step-by-step practical guides in deploying Horizon Workspace and its key features and functionalities in a lab environment. If you want to work through the practical examples, you will need the following infrastructure:

- 1 vCenter Server
- 1 ESXi host server with:
    ◦ A minimum of 8 cores
    ◦ 16 GB RAM
    ◦ 500 GB of local or SAN-attached storage
- Windows Server 2008 R2 Active Directory with DNS configured
- VMware Horizon Suite, which offers the following components:
    ◦ Horizon Workspace 1.5
    ◦ Horizon View 5.3
    ◦ ThinApp (packages created for Horizon Workspace)
- Salesforce.com developer account (required for SaaS integration)
- iOS Device (iPhone or iPad)
- Android smartphone (VMware Ready device and/or Android device)

Who this book is for

This book is aimed at IT professionals who are relatively new to the Horizon Workspace product, looking to understand the technology at a deeper level and how it will help deliver end-user environments. It will explain how the technology works, how to set it up, and then how to get started with deploying and managing the key features and functionalities.

It will guide you through the best practices in designing a Horizon Workspace solution, both for production installations and in proof of concept and pilot environments.

At the end of this book, you will have built the skills and knowledge to design, configure, install, and manage a Horizon Workspace infrastructure to deliver the tools a user needs to get their job done.

Conventions

In this book, you will find a number of styles of text that distinguish between different kinds of information. Here are some examples of these styles, and an explanation of their meaning.

Code words in text are shown as follows: "Log in to Horizon Workspace using `testuser2`, as shown in the following screenshot:"

Any command-line input or output is written as follows:

```
VMware-Horizon -Workspace-1.x.x-XXXX.exe /v ENABLE_DATA=0
```

New terms and **important words** are shown in bold. Words that you see on the screen, in menus or dialog boxes for example, appear in the text like this: "If something is not correct or you need to make a change later, simply click on **Edit** to change the settings."

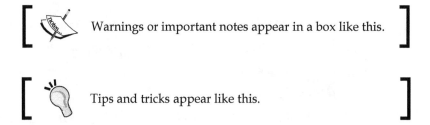

> Warnings or important notes appear in a box like this.

> Tips and tricks appear like this.

Reader feedback

Feedback from our readers is always welcome. Let us know what you think about this book—what you liked or may have disliked. Reader feedback is important for us to develop titles that you really get the most out of.

To send us general feedback, simply send an e-mail to `feedback@packtpub.com`, and mention the book title via the subject of your message. If there is a topic that you have expertise in and you are interested in either writing or contributing to a book, see our author guide on `www.packtpub.com/authors`.

Customer support

Now that you are the proud owner of a Packt book, we have a number of things to help you to get the most from your purchase.

Errata

Although we have taken every care to ensure the accuracy of our content, mistakes do happen. If you find a mistake in one of our books—maybe a mistake in the text or the code—we would be grateful if you would report this to us. By doing so, you can save other readers from frustration and help us improve subsequent versions of this book. If you find any errata, please report them by visiting http://www.packtpub. com/submit-errata, selecting your book, clicking on the **errata submission form** link, and entering the details of your errata. Once your errata are verified, your submission will be accepted and the errata will be uploaded on our website, or added to any list of existing errata, under the Errata section of that title. Any existing errata can be viewed by selecting your title from http://www.packtpub.com/support.

Piracy

Piracy of copyright material on the Internet is an ongoing problem across all media. At Packt, we take the protection of our copyright and licenses very seriously. If you come across any illegal copies of our works, in any form, on the Internet, please provide us with the location address or website name immediately so that we can pursue a remedy.

Please contact us at copyright@packtpub.com with a link to the suspected pirated material.

We appreciate your help in protecting our authors, and our ability to bring you valuable content.

Questions

You can contact us at questions@packtpub.com if you are having a problem with any aspect of the book, and we will do our best to address it.

1
Getting Started with VMware Horizon Workspace

In this chapter, we will introduce you to VMware Horizon Workspace, where it is positioned in the market, and then give you an overview of all the components you need before starting to deploy the technology.

We will also cover where you can download the software from, outline the time requirements to install and configure a successful deployment, and give tips on what to think about for a full production environment. This book is primarily geared towards a test environment, as that's where most projects start. However, we will provide hints, tips, and best practices on building, delivering, and administering a full production environment as well.

Introduction to VMware Horizon Workspace

Horizon Workspace is a new type of solution that is commonly referred to as **Workspace Aggregator**. A solution that provides end users with a single point of access to their corporate data, applications, and other IT resources, as well as providing IT administrators with a single point of administration.

Let's first discuss the background and challenges that exist in most corporations today.

There are some ongoing technology trends that will affect us all and how we deliver IT services to our end users. A few of these are as follows:

- BYOD
- Software-as-a-Service

- Mobile applications
- Mobile/tablet devices
- Always on network connectivity
- Consumerization

In the last few years, the market has exploded with new devices, applications, and services that have been focused on being easy to pick up and consume with little technical knowledge.

Companies such as Google, Apple, Facebook, Twitter, and Dropbox have had enormous adoption with consumers; all of these services offer a great user experience and is easy to use.

For a long time, corporate IT companies have been able to withstand the pressure from these trends by locking environments down and mandating what users can access by way of applying policies, but we have reached a point where users are starting to circumnavigate these policies and utilize these services directly and not involving the corporate IT department and its policies. This is commonly referred to as **shadow IT**.

The traditional approach has been to deploy Windows on physical machines, and use some form of a distribution system for deploying applications and securing data. Users typically work between 8 a.m. and 5 p.m., usually from the office, and as the computers are physically attached to the desk, it's been considered secure.

Corporate IT risks turning into a slow moving dinosaur that does not contribute, but rather hinders innovation and users' ability to be productive. Users are starting to avoid involving IT since it takes a long time and is slow moving. There is now a real threat that corporate IT becomes irrelevant thanks to the competition from these outside trends.

Some real examples we have seen is when a business unit goes out and buys a solution somewhere from the Internet and is not even involving corporate IT since it would make the process slower and less productive.

Another common example is when users are using consumer-based file sharing applications to be able to share information or collaborate with partners, internal or external, to their organization.

When exposed to these threats, the following are the three common typical reactions:

- Ignore it!

  Pretending that your users are not using these services and devices is a sure way of getting a false sense of security and comfort

- Lock it down!

  Tightening the control even more usually forces people to find ways around the systems and will make the users unhappy

- Implement a point solution

  Just solving one of the challenges might buy you some time, but in the end will actually increase the complexity since there will be many point solutions to solve all the challenges

Another approach is to embrace the advances in technology and to listen to the users' requests. This is where VMware Horizon Workspace can help.

Horizon Workspace addresses these new challenges, such as delivering web applications, mobile applications, and data collaboration to any device. The key point to highlight is that you can give the users the tools and the modern approach that they have become used to as a consumer, but still retain security and control.

Horizon Workspace 1.5 provides the following functionalities:

- A single workspace for apps and data
- Anywhere, anytime access
- Data synchronization
- Separate personal and corporate data
- A virtualized container for Android devices
- Native application support
- Detailed policy management
- Simple user and application management
- Share files seamlessly and securely
- Enterprise-grade security
- Complete on-premise solutions
- Access controls

So what is the business value for a customer when they deploy this solution? We can divide this into two aspects: one for end users and one for corporate IT.

- For end users:
  - Easy access to applications, files, and virtual desktops
  - Single Sign-On to internal and external web-based applications
  - One place to access all services

- ° A service catalog where the users can quickly get access to new services
- ° Own choice of device and networks to work from
- ° Use multiple devices without complex configurations or VPN
- ° Sanctioned way to share files and collaborate with internal and external parties

- For corporate IT:
  - ° Common model on how to entitle and disentitle users to services
  - ° Faster time to market for new services
  - ° Stop worrying about devices and start managing users
  - ° Extensible platform that can be integrated into existing services
  - ° Common reporting for all types of applications

Ease of deployment

Horizon Workspace comes packaged as a vApp, which means that it's a number of preconfigured virtual machines in a container with the extension .ova. **Open Virtual Appliance (OVA)** is a standard way of packaging a vApp.

It needs to be deployed using VMware vCenter Server on to a VMware vSphere virtualization platform. We will cover the prerequisites later in this chapter.

The benefits with this type of deployment is many, since the vApp is preinstalled with the operating system (Horizon Workspace is based on Suse Linux Enterprise Server) and all components that make up Horizon Workspace. The only thing you need to do is to configure the unique settings for your environment. There is no complicated operating system to install and configure, and no installer to run.

Just download and deploy.

Another benefit of being deployed within a virtual environment is that we can take advantage of all the features that the virtual infrastructure platform provides for, which are high availability, load balancing, backup, and disaster recovery.

Proving the technology

Before embarking on a **Proof of Concept** (**POC**) or Pilot of Horizon Workspace, the following are a few things that we have learned from our experience in working with the technology:

- Do not run a POC/Pilot on production systems
    - ° This could possibly interfere with your running systems
- Do not run a POC/Pilot using production applications.
    - ° Horizon Workspace can take over the authentication for web-based applications that it integrates with and can disable other ways of authenticating, potentially locking out other users
- Make sure that you have clearly defined the success criteria. It's hard to know whether you have succeeded if there are no clear goals or objectives defined

Now that we have introduced you to VMware Horizon Workspace, we are going to cover what you need to get your environment up and running in the following sections.

Prerequisites

The first thing we are going to cover are the prerequisites in more details. We will start with the test environment first.

Infrastructure requirements for an initial test setup

You will need the following hardware and virtual infrastructure components:

- 1 vCenter Server
- 1 ESXi host server with:
    - ° A minimum of 8 cores
    - ° 14 GB RAM
    - ° 412 GB of local disk or SAN attached storage

The installation and configuration of vCenter and ESXi is beyond the scope of this book and therefore we assume that you already will have this in place.

 Using VMware Workstation or VMware Fusion natively does not work since the vApp requires a vCenter to be able to deploy. As an alternative, you could use something known as **nested hypervisors**. This means that you can use VMware Workstation or Fusion and create a virtual vCenter and virtual instance of ESXi. Be aware though that this will cause considerable overhead and require a powerful CPU, plenty of memory, and a fast disk system.

Infrastructure requirements for production deployment

For production environments, you will need the following minimum hardware and virtual infrastructure components:

- 1 vCenter-server, redundant
- 2 ESXi-hosts (3 ESXi hosts are recommended)
- 500 GB of SAN storage
- Network Load balancer
- NFS-storage for Horizon Files

Horizon Workspace supports a number of VMware vSphere versions listed as follows:

- vCenter: 5.0 U2, 5.1, and 5.5
- ESXi: 5.0 U2, 5.1, and 5.5

When setting up your ESXi hosts, ensure that you configure them to use the **Network Time Protocol (NTP)**. Correct time synchronization is critical for a successful installation since the SAML-based authentication is based on short-lived assertions of 60 seconds. If there is a time difference, logins will fail.

Network, DNS, and Active Directory requirements

The initial deployment of Horizon Workspace will require 5 IP addresses. If you need redundancy and external access, you will need additional IP addresses. Each of the IP's need a static DNS host record as well as reverse pointer-records (PTR record).

DNS name resolution needs to be fully implemented for both forward and reverse lookups. Horizon Workspace will not function without reverse lookups configured.

For this book, we have used Windows Server 2008 R2 Active Directory and DNS; however, Horizon Workspace supports Windows 2003 Active Directory or later. Using Bind DNS will work just as well as using Microsoft DNS.

As we go through the setup of the **Active Directory (AD)** infrastructure to support our installation, it's worth making a note of some of the key information that you will be prompted for during the actual configuration process. Make a note of the following information:

- Name of the Active Directory controller
- **Fully qualified domain name (FQDN)** of the Active Directory controller
- Base DN— the container from where to start searching for users; in our example, this would be something like ou=horizon, dc=domain_name, or dc=local
- The Bind DN username and password
- Administrator account or an account with rights to add computers to the domain

> The Bind DN username is an account that will be used to communicate with Active Directory to read user information and their attributes. The Bind DN will become the first administrator in your Horizon Workspace installation. In our examples, we have set up a Horizon Administrator account to do this. You need to enter the details in the following format:
>
> cn=horizonadmin,ou=horizon,dc=domain_name,dc=local

vCenter Server requirements

Before installing the vApp, you need to configure an IP pool for the Horizon Workspace vApp that contains the correct IP address range along with details of your DNS server (you can only specify one DNS server). You also need the name of the domain into which you will deploy your VMs.

> IP pools are used by vCenter to provide a network identity to vApps. The IP pool itself is a network configuration that you assign to a network used by the vApp. Once set up, the vApp can use vCenter to provide the IP configuration to the virtual machines it contains.

External access

For users to log on to their Workspace, you will need to make sure certain network ports are open. For external access, you will need to ensure that the TCP port 443 is open for the connector-va appliance to communicate. For a production environment with a **demilitarized zone (DMZ)** — a term for a network between internal and external networks — and connection to external services such as Active Directory and RSA SecureID, additional ports may need to be opened. If you are also integrating with Horizon View, you will need to make sure that those ports are also open.

Certificates

For a production environment, you will need publicly signed certificates from a trusted certificate provider. For a test environment, you can use a self-signed certificate. The certificate must have the FQDN of your Horizon Workspace installation as the **Subject Alternative Name (SAN)** of the certificate or you can use a Wildcard certificate.

Horizon Workspace vApp

Horizon Workspace comes packaged as a vApp, which means that it's a number of preconfigured virtual machines in a single file with the extension OVA. (The OVA extension is a standard way of packaging a vApp).

There are many benefits with this type of deployment. The vApp is preinstalled with the operating system (Horizon Workspace is based on **SUSE Enterprise Linux (SLES)**) along with all the components that make up Horizon Workspace. The only thing you need to do is to configure the unique settings in your environment. There is no operating system to install and no installer to run.

Use a naming convention that makes sense to you and is consistent throughout your environment. For a test environment you can keep the default appliance names, but for production, it would make sense to name them, so that they are meaningful to your environment and also as one of the appliances will be the address that your users will use to connect.

Choose your hostnames and enter them into your DNS server along with the associated IP addresses. During the installation process, the appliances will perform a reverse lookup in DNS to determine (resolve) what their hostname is.

An overview of vApp

As we previously discussed, Horizon Workspace is comprised of five virtual appliances as shown in the following diagram:

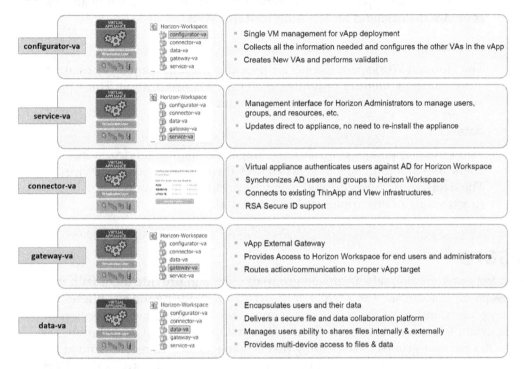

The five virtual appliances (va) are described in the following list:

- **gateway-va**

   The Horizon Workspace Gateway is the single entity for all end user communication. All user requests hit the **gateway-va** virtual machine, which then routes the request to the appropriate virtual appliance. The Gateway appliance offers a single namespace for accessing the Horizon Workspace implementation.

- **configurator-va**

   Horizon Workspace is configured using this virtual appliance, so this appliance configures all the other appliances. It has both a console and a web interface. Any configuration changes you make with the configurator are then distributed to the other virtual appliances within the vApp automatically, for example, SSL-certificates and root passwords.

- **service-va**

  Horizon Workspace uses a standard named SAML for authentication of users and to extend the identities, which is explained in more detail in *Chapter 4, Integrating SaaS Applications*. The **service-va** controls this function and also provides the frontend for the Administrator Web interface.

- **connector-va**

  The Horizon Workspace Connector provides the following services: user authentication (identity provider), directory synchronization, ThinApp synchronization, and View pool synchronization.

- **data-va**

  This virtual appliance controls file storage and sharing service, stores users' files and folders, and synchronizes them across multiple devices. The **data-va** also hosts the end user web portal. We will cover the functionality of this appliance in *Chapter 3, Horizon Files*.

Users

For a test environment, select a mixed group of users and provide them with the necessary equipment such as a tablet or an extra phone during the test phase. To get a good understanding of the solution and how users will consume the services, it is important to expose a few users from different departments to the solution. Try to restrict the user groups to something that is manageable; we recommend at least five, but no more than 10 in the first phase. Once you move into production, Horizon Workspace will affect all of your users as it becomes the central place they log on to in order to access the tools, data, and applications to get their job done. This is likely to be a major change from how they work today.

Allow time and resources for user training and use your Pilot users as **Horizon Workspace Champions**. They can then manage the initial user issues.

Downloading the software

An easy way of finding the software is to browse the VMware's official portal at https://my.vmware.com.

Now, navigate to **Downloads** | **All Products**. From there, scroll down to **Desktop & End-User Computing** and find the **VMware Horizon Workspace** entry.

Simply click on **View Download Components | Product Downloads | VMware Horizon Workspace | Go to Downloads**. From there, find the VMware Horizon Workspace and click on **Download Now**.

Unless you are already logged in, you will be asked to provide your username and password for your My VMware account. If you do not have one, register a new account.

If you receive a message saying that you are not entitled to this download, it means that no licenses are registered to your account. If you have not purchased any licenses, you can request an evaluation license instead. To do this, perform the following steps:

1. Click on **Download Trial**.
2. Click on **Register** and complete the required information and then click on **Continue**.

Take a note of your license information and then proceed to the download.

 Since it's a big download, about 5.2 GB, please verify the MD5SUM or SHA1SUM once the download is complete with the one published on the download page. An incomplete/corrupt download could cause unpredictable problems later.

Summary

In this chapter, we have introduced you to Horizon Workspace and the major trends for end-user computing and the challenges associated with them.

We have also learned about the major components of VMware Horizon Workspace and the prerequisites and pieces you need to deploy the solution.

In the next chapter, we will cover the installation of the Horizon Workspace vApp and the configuration steps.

2
Design, Install, and Configure

In this chapter, we will cover the basic installation and configuration of Horizon Workspace 1.5. After making sure all the prerequisites are in place, we can now deploy the Horizon Workspace vApp.

In this chapter, we will cover the following key subjects:

- Horizon Workspace Architecture Overview
- Designing a solution
- Sizing guidelines
- vApp deployment
- Step-by-step configuration
- Install Certificates
- Setting up Kerberos **Single Sign-On (SSO)**

Reading this chapter will provide you with an introduction to the solution, and also provides you with useful reference points throughout the book that will help you install, configure, and manage a Horizon Workspace deployment. A few things are out of scope for this chapter, such as setting up vSphere, configuring HA, and using certificates. We will assume that the core infrastructure is already in place.

We start by looking at the solution architecture and then how to size a deployment, based on best practice, and suitable to meet the requirements of your end users. Next we will cover the preparation steps in vCenter and then deploy the Horizon Workspace vApp.

There are then two steps to installation and configuration. First we will guide you through the initial command-line-based setup and then finally the web-based Setup Wizard. Each section is described in easy to follow steps, and shown in detail using actual screenshots of our lab deployment.

So let's get started with the architecture overview.

The Horizon Workspace architecture

The following diagram shows a more detailed view of how the architecture fits together:

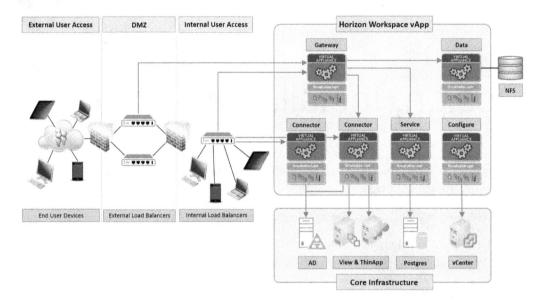

The Horizon Workspace sizing guide

We have already discussed that Horizon Workspace is made up of five virtual appliances. However, for production environments, you will need to deploy multiple instances to provide for high availability, offer load balancing, and support the number of users that you need in your environment.

For a **Proof of Concept (POC)** or pilot deployment, this is of less importance.

Sizing the Horizon Workspace virtual appliances

The following diagram shows the maximum number of users that each appliance can accommodate. Using these maximum values, you can calculate the number of appliances that you need to deploy.

	connector-va	gateway-va	service-va	data-va	configurator-va
	2 x vCPU	6 x vCPU	6 x vCPU	6 x vCPU	1 x vCPU
	4 GB RAM	32 GB RAM	8 GB RAM	32 GB RAM	1 GB RAM
	5 GB	9 GB	32 GB	175 GB*	5 GB
	30,000 Users	2,000 Users	100,000 Users	1,000 Users	N/A

* Does not include storage for users data

For example, if you had 6,000 users in your environment, you would need to deploy a single **connector-va** appliance, three **gateway-va** appliances, one **service-va** appliance, seven **data-va** appliances, and a single **configurator-va** appliance. Please note that data-va should be sized using *N+1*. The first data-va appliance should never contain any user data. For high availability, you may want to use two connector-va appliances and two service-va appliances.

Sizing for Preview services

If you plan to use a Microsoft Preview Server, this needs to be sized based on the requirements shown in the following diagram:

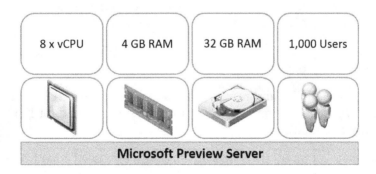

8 x vCPU	4 GB RAM	32 GB RAM	1,000 Users

Microsoft Preview Server

If we use our previous example of 6,000 users, then to use Microsoft Preview, you would require a total of six Microsoft Preview Servers. Microsoft Preview services are covered in more detail in *Chapter 3, Horizon Files*.

The Horizon Workspace database

You have a few options for the database.

For a POC or pilot environment, you can use the internal database functionality. In a production deployment, you would use an external database option, using either VMware PostgreSQL or Oracle 11g. This allows you to have a highly available and protected database.

The VMware recommendation is PostgreSQL, and the following diagram details the sizing information for the Horizon Workspace database:

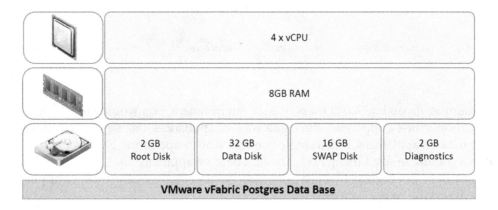

External access and load balancing considerations

In a production environment, high availability, redundancy, and external access is a core requirement. This needs planning and configuration.

For a POC or pilot deployment, this is usually not of high importance but should be something to be aware of.

To achieve high availability and redundancy, a load balancer is required in front of the gateway-va and the connector-va appliances that are used for Kerberos (Windows authentication).

If external access is required, then typically you will also need a load balancer in the **Demilitarized Zone** (**DMZ**). This is detailed in the diagram at the beginning of this chapter.

It is not supported to place gateway-va appliances in the DMZ.

For more detailed information about load balancing, please visit the following guide:

```
https://communities.vmware.com/docs/DOC-24577
```

Deploying and configuring the vApp

After the last chapter, you should be familiar with the vApp concept, the virtual appliances within it, and how it is delivered.

The installation is a three-stage process:

- vApp deployment in vCenter
- Command-line configuration and setup of virtual appliances
- Browser-based setup wizard for directory integration and users

To start the process, we need to launch the vCenter Client and choose to deploy the Horizon Workspace vApp. In this example, we will use the Windows-based vCenter Client, but you could also use the vSphere Web Client.

Configuring an IP pool

Before we actually deploy the vApp, we first need to configure an IP pool for the Horizon Workspace vApp. To do this, follow the steps as described in the following screenshot:

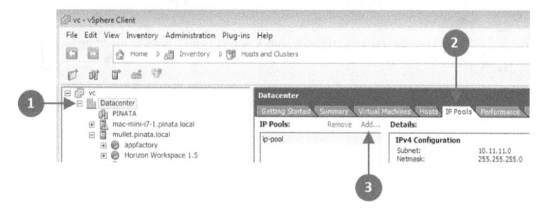

From the vSphere Client, click on the **Datacenter** to deploy the vApp to (**1**), click on the **IP Pools** tab (**2**), and then click on **Add...** (**3**), as shown in the previous screenshot.

Enter the information for the IP pool as shown in the following screenshot:

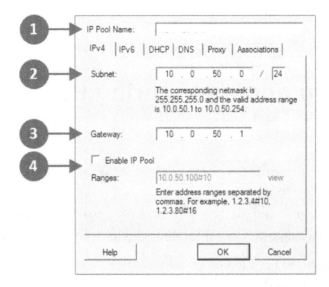

Use the following steps to enter the details:

1. Enter a name for the IP pool (**1**), for example, "Horizon Workspace".
2. Enter the IP address (**2**) for the subnet that you want the virtual appliances to use.
3. Enter the IP address of your Gateway (**3**).
4. Make sure *not* to tick the **Enable IP Pool** checkbox (**4**).

 The last option is only to assign a pool of IP addresses to the IP pool; we will not use that functionality, since we need static addresses.

Click on **OK** when you have completed entering the information for the IP pool.

For the next part of the configuration, click on the **DNS** tab at the top (**1**) as shown in the following screenshot:

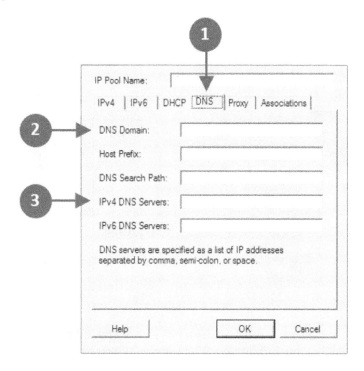

Enter the information for the DNS configuration as shown in the previous screenshot.

Enter your DNS Domain (**2**) and your IPv4 DNS Server (**3**).

The final and most important part is to associate the newly created IP pool with the virtual network that the Horizon Workspace virtual appliances will use, as shown in the following screenshot.

Click on the **Associations** tab at the top (**1**) and then check the boxes (**2**) for the network(s) that you want to use this IP pool.

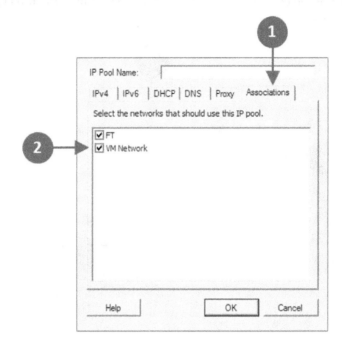

Click on **OK** when you have finished. You have now created the IP pool, and we can move on to the next stage and deploy the Horizon Workspace vApp.

Deploying the vApp

Now deploy the vApp as shown in the following screenshot.

First, click on **File** (**1**) from the top menu and then select **Deploy OVF Template…** (**2**).

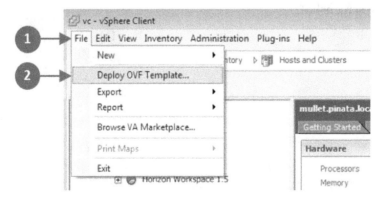

You will see the **Deploy OVF Template** dialog box as shown in the next screenshot. The first thing is to enter the location for the Horizon Workspace vApp OVF file (**1**), or click on **Browse** (**2**) to search for it in another location. You can either deploy from a file or a URL. If you followed the instructions in *Chapter 1, Getting Started with VMware Horizon Workspace*, you should have this file already downloaded.

Click on **Next >** once you have entered the location, as shown in the following screenshot:

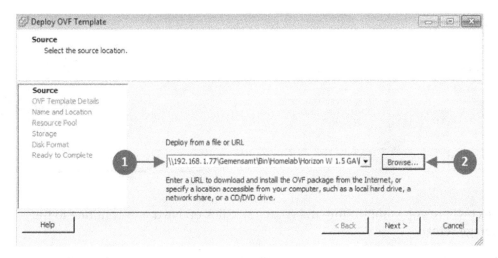

You will now see the details of the template displayed, showing the size of the download and disk space required for deployment. Click on **Next >** to continue.

On the **End-User License Agreement** (**EULA**) screen, click on the **Accept** button to accept the EULA, and then click on **Next >** to continue to the **Name and Location** screen, as shown in the following screenshot:

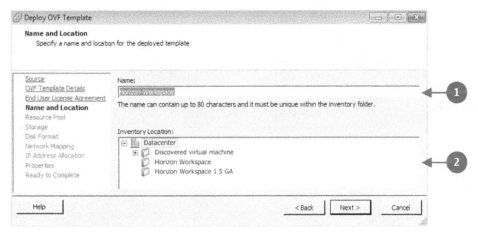

Enter a name for the template (**1**). This is what the vApp will be called in vCenter.

Choose a location where you want the vApp to be deployed (**2**). Click on **Next >** to continue to the **Resource Pool** screen, shown in the following screenshot:

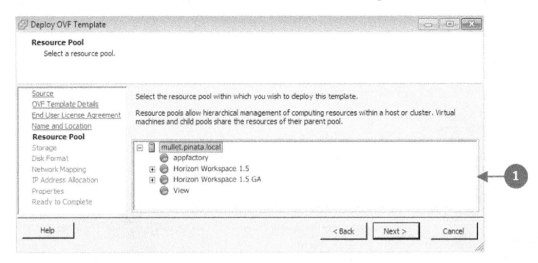

Select where you want to store the vApp (**1**). Click on **Next >** to continue to the **Storage** screen.

From the **Storage** screen, select a data store that has enough disk space to host the virtual appliances. Click on **Next >** to continue to the **Disk Format** screen, as shown in the following screenshot:

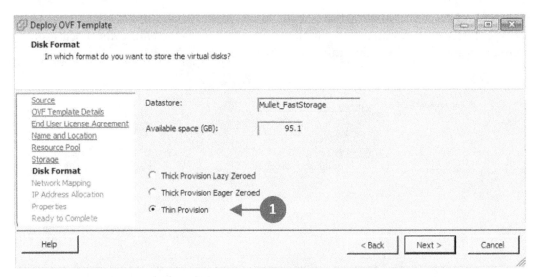

Click on the radio button for **Thin Provision** (1) (shown in the previous screenshot), and then click on **Next >** to continue to the **Network Mapping** screen, as shown in the following screenshot:

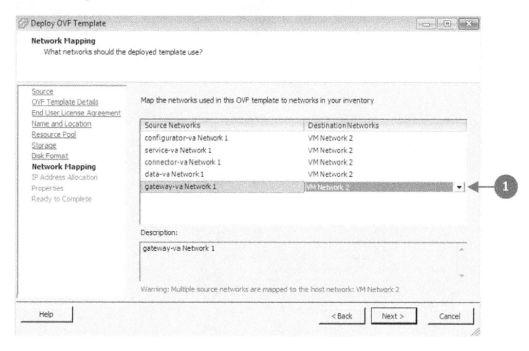

For each Horizon Workspace virtual appliance listed, highlight one at a time, click on the arrow for the drop-down menu (**1**), and select the appropriate network.

 If you have determined that you need more virtual appliances for capacity, redundancy, or load balancing, don't worry, we will configure these later.

Click on **Next >** to continue to the **IP Address Allocation** screen. Click on the radio button for **Fixed** and ensure that you have selected **IPv4** from the drop-down menu. Click on **Next >** to continue to the **Properties** screen, as shown in the following screenshot.

On the **Properties** screen, we are going to enter the IP address for each of the Horizon Workspace virtual appliances.

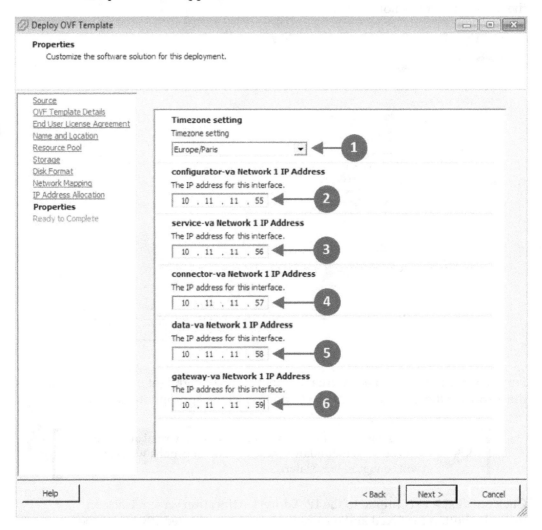

First, from the drop-down menu (**1**), select your time zone. Next, enter the IP address that you have allocated for each of the virtual appliances (**2 – 6**). There are five in total, as shown in the previous screenshot.

 This is why it is critical to have reverse lookup set up correctly in your DNS. As part of the deployment of the vApp, the IP addresses will be resolved to find the hostname of each appliance.

Click on **Next >** to continue to the **Ready to Complete** screen.

Review the information and check the **Power on after deployment** box. Click on **Finish** to complete the wizard and the vApp will start to deploy, as shown in the following screenshot:

You can monitor the progress of the deployment in the task manager in the vSphere Client (shown in the previous screenshot). Once it's completed, you should see the following screenshot:

At this stage, if you had ticked the **Power on after deployment** box, you would only see that the configurator-va appliance is powered on. This would also be the case if you powered on the vApp.

Do not power on any of the other appliances. As part of this next process, the configurator-va appliance will power on and configure the other appliances in the vApp.

The next step is to continue the installation using the command-line configuration, as described in the next section.

The command-line configuration process

The first thing that we need to do is open a console onto the configurator-va virtual appliance. From the vSphere Client, browse to the Horizon Workspace vApp and locate the configurator-va appliance. Right-click on it and select **Open Console**. You will see the following screenshot. Verify that you have the information needed to complete the configuration.

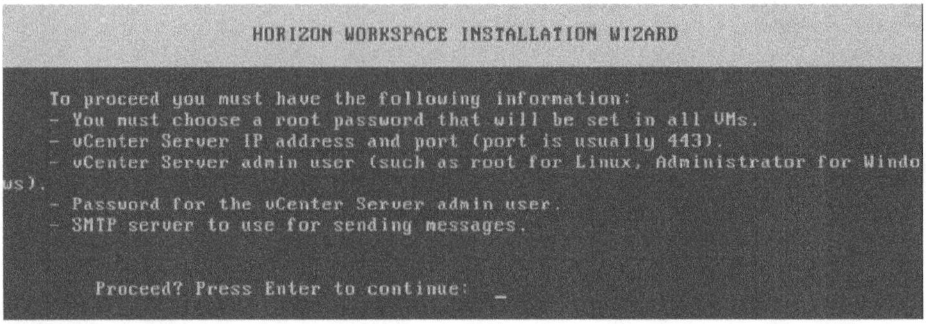

```
                    HORIZON WORKSPACE INSTALLATION WIZARD


        To proceed you must have the following information:
         - You must choose a root password that will be set in all VMs.
         - vCenter Server IP address and port (port is usually 443).
         - vCenter Server admin user (such as root for Linux, Administrator for Windo
ws).
         - Password for the vCenter Server admin user.
         - SMTP server to use for sending messages.


            Proceed? Press Enter to continue:  _
```

Press *Enter* to start the installation process.

There will first be an automated verification of the IP addresses configured in the vApp setup. If this process fails and hostnames cannot be resolved, then the installation process will stop and return an error. If that happens, go back and verify that the DNS is set up correctly and the IP pool is associated with the right network.

In the following screenshot, you can see an example of a successful verification. The IP addresses should have been resolved and the installation can continue.

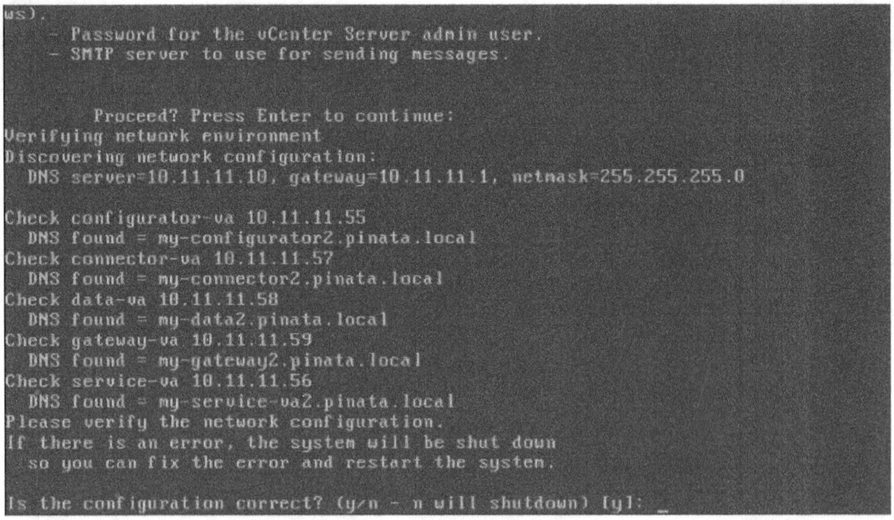

```
ws).
         - Password for the vCenter Server admin user.
         - SMTP server to use for sending messages.


            Proceed? Press Enter to continue:
Verifying network environment
Discovering network configuration:
  DNS server=10.11.11.10, gateway=10.11.11.1, netmask=255.255.255.0

Check configurator-va 10.11.11.55
  DNS found = my-configurator2.pinata.local
Check connector-va 10.11.11.57
  DNS found = my-connector2.pinata.local
Check data-va 10.11.11.58
  DNS found = my-data2.pinata.local
Check gateway-va 10.11.11.59
  DNS found = my-gateway2.pinata.local
Check service-va 10.11.11.56
  DNS found = my-service-va2.pinata.local
Please verify the network configuration.
If there is an error, the system will be shut down
  so you can fix the error and restart the system.

Is the configuration correct? (y/n - n will shutdown) [y]: _
```

If the information is correct, then press *Enter*. If not, then as we mentioned previously, the installation will halt.

Next, you will now be asked to enter the following information:

- A global root password that is used for all the virtual appliances in the vApp
- A DNS name and port number for your SMTP server

 The setup requires a valid SMTP server to be entered, and you won't be able to continue the process without it. Just to get on with the deployment, you can point to your configurator-va virtual machine. You can change the SMTP server settings once you have set up the vApp.

- The IP address or hostname of your vCenter Server, port number, username, and password

Verify that the information is correct and press *Enter*, as shown in the following screenshot:

```
Enter SMTP port number [25]:

This VM registers itself as vCenter Server Extension. Once registered, it will h
ave full access to the vCenter Server inventory.
This VM will manage other VMs in the vApp. To register as a vCenter Server Exten
sion, vCenter Server credentials are needed.
Please enter vCenter Server credentials below:

Enter vCenter Server IP Address or hostname []: vc.pinata.local
Enter vCenter Server port [443]:
Enter vCenter Server admin user [root]:
Enter vCenter Server admin password:
Verifying vCenter Server connection details...


    Global root:           ***
    SMTP Server:           my-configurator2.pinata.local:25

    vCenter Server:        vc.pinata.local
    vCenter Server port:   443
    vCenter Server user:   root
    vCenter Server pass:   ***


    Is this correct? (y/n) [y]: _
```

The configuration will take a few minutes, and if successful, the following screenshot should be displayed. The key piece of information on this screen is the URL for the CA Cert. Remember to take a note of this URL. You may need this if you use a load balancer.

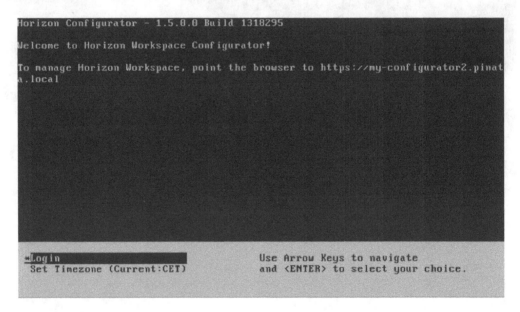

```
Configuring Connector VMs
Configuring connector-va VM.
Startup time configuration done successfully.

Success
Configuring internal SSL certificates for VMs
 Configuring FQDN on Gateway
Configuring firewall rules for VMs
Starting web app, please wait...
Gateway Initialization
....................................................
Gateway initialization successful
Verifying Application Manager is running...

Application Manager connection test succeeded.

Success!

Horizon Workspace CA Cert for reverse proxy/load balancer
available at:
    http://my-gateway2.pinata.local/horizon_workspace_rootca.pem


    Press Enter to continue
```

If you now press *Enter*, you will see the main Horizon Workspace Configurator screen, as shown in the following screenshot. From here, you are able to log in to the command-line interface or set the time zone.

```
Horizon Configurator - 1.5.0.0 Build 1318295

Welcome to Horizon Workspace Configurator!

To manage Horizon Workspace, point the browser to https://my-configurator2.pinat
a.local




 *Login                                         Use Arrow Keys to navigate
  Set Timezone (Current:CET)                    and <ENTER> to select your choice.
```

We have now completed the vApp deployment and the command-line configuration process. The next stage of the configuration is browser-based; to log on to the configurator, you would use the URL shown on the main screen as displayed in the previous screenshot.

Web-based configuration

Once you have completed the CLI-based configuration, we can move on to the Web-based part. Start by opening a browser and enter the URL to the configurator-va appliance.

You should see **Welcome to Horizon Workspace!** as shown in the following screenshot:

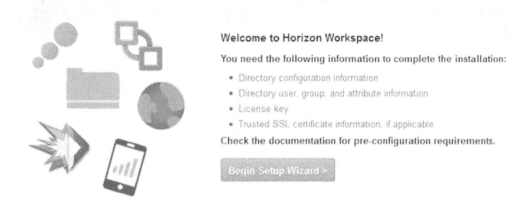

Click on the green **Begin Setup Wizard >** button to start.

You will now see the **Step 1: Setup** screen as shown in the following screenshot:

Enter the following information:

- **License Key (1)**: If you are using evaluation licenses, the expiry date will be displayed. It's a good idea to take note of this date so that this does not come up as a surprise later!

- **Password (2)**: This is the password for the Horizon Workspace admin account, which is *not* the AD service account. This is the account used for administering the configurator-va appliance.

- **Confirm Password (3)**: Confirm the password for the admin account.

Click on **Next >** to continue to the **Step 2: Configure** screen.

The dialog box displayed in the previous screenshot reminds you of the information that you need to complete the configuration. Click on **Continue with the Setup Wizard >** to continue to the **Step 2a: Database Connection Setup** screen.

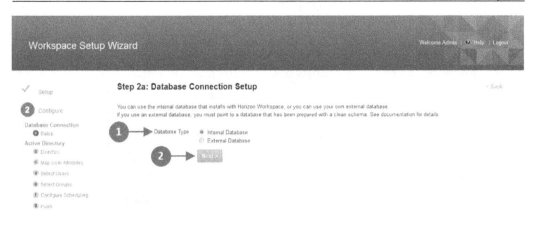

Select the **Database Type** (**1**) that you want to use, as shown in the previous screenshot. In our example and for a POC deployment, the internal database is sufficient.

For the production deployments, you would use an external database that can provide high availability and redundancy. Click on **Next >** (**2**) for the next step, which is shown in the following screenshot:

Enter the following information:

- From the drop-down menu (**1**), choose the directory type
- Enter the FQDN or IP address of your directory server (**2**)
- Check the box (**3**), if SSL is used to connect to the directory server
- Enter the directory server port number (**4**) (the default for **Lightweight Directory Access Protocol** (**LDAP**) is 389)
- From the drop-down menu (**5**), select the attribute in the directory that contains the username (the default for AD is **sAMAccountName**)
- Enter the **Base DN** that is the starting point in the directory, from where to start searching for users
- Enter the **Bind DN** that is the directory-based administrator/service account, and will also be the first administrator in Horizon Workspace
- Enter the password for the directory-based administrator/service account

Click on **Next >** to continue to the **Map User Attributes** configuration screen, as shown in the following screenshot:

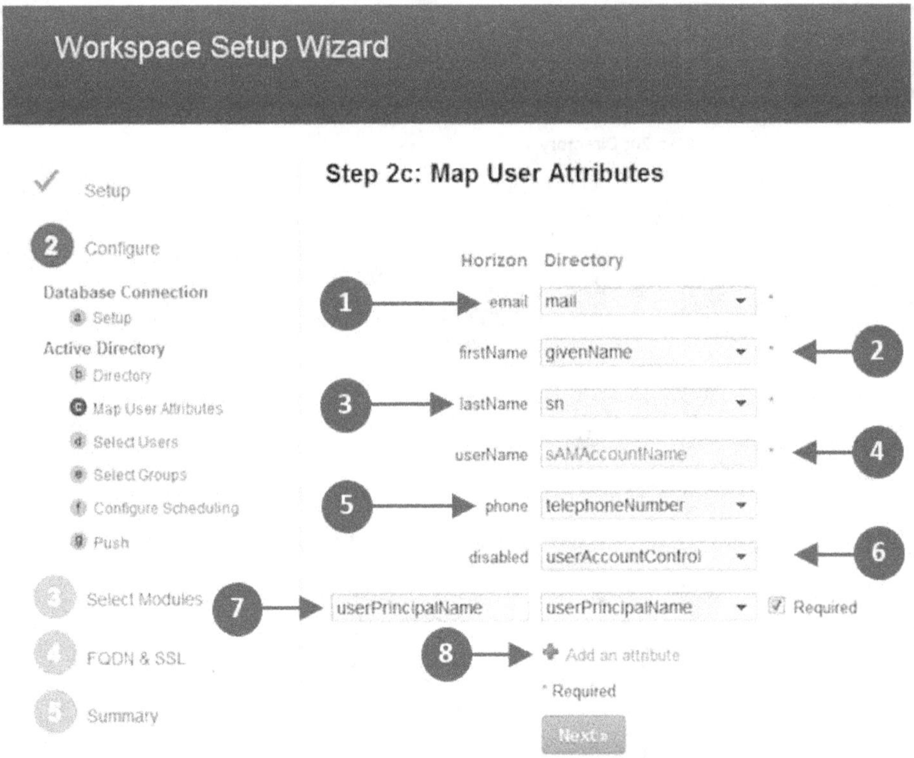

Enter the following information to map the directory details to match the Horizon Workspace attributes:

- **email (1)**: The **mail** attribute in the Active Directory.

- **firstName (2)**: The **givenName** attribute in the Active Directory.

- **lastName (3)**: The **sn** attribute in the Active Directory.

- **userName (4)**: The **sAMAccountName** attribute in the Active Directory.

- **phone (5)**: The **telephoneNumber** attribute in the Active Directory (this is optional).

- **disabled (6)**: The **userAccountControl** attribute in the Active Directory (this is optional).

- **userPrincipalName (7)**: The **userPrincipalName** attribute in the Active Directory (this is optional but recommended). This attribute is used for the Horizon View integration. We will discuss this in more detail in *Chapter 7, Horizon View Integration*.

Click on **Next >** to continue to the **Select Users** screen:

Enter the DN for the location of your users (**1**), as shown in the previous screenshot. You can add an additional DN by clicking on **+ Add DN** (**2**).

You can use the filters to narrow your search results by excluding particular details (**3**). For example, you could exclude the users whose name contains "Peter". You can add an additional filter (**4**) if required.

Once you have completed the details, click on **Refresh Results** (5). To see the results, click on the **View Results** tab (6). This screen will contain all the users that will be synchronized.

[The administrator account needs to be one of the accounts that are synchronized. If it fails to be synchronized or is removed, then you will not be able to log in and manage Horizon Workspace.]

Click on **Next >** to continue to the **Select Groups** screen, as shown in the following screenshot:

Enter the DN for Groups (**1**): these are the **Organizational Unit (OU)** groups where your Horizon Workspace users sit within the directory structure. Click on **Search** (**2**) to find the groups. You can specify an additional DN by clicking on **+ Add DN** (**3**).

 Horizon Workspace has support for Horizon Workspace internal groups. These groups are very flexible because you can assign membership based on filter rules. If you still want to entitle users based on Active Directory group membership, you must select these Active Directory groups in your Directory Sync.

Click on **Next >** to continue to the **Configure Scheduling** screen.

From the drop-down menu, select the frequency that Horizon Workspace should synchronize with the directory. You have the options of **Weekly**, **Daily**, **Hourly**, and **Manually**. The default setting is **Hourly**.

Click on **Next >** to continue to the **Push to Horizon** screen, as shown in the following screenshot:

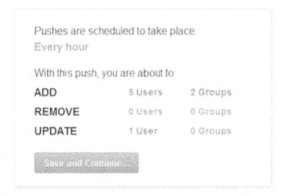

Verify that this is the expected number of users and groups that will be synchronized. If the number of users are more or less than you expected, then go back and verify that the Base DN is correct. Particularly, check any users or groups that are being removed, especially if it is the administrator account.

Click on **Save and Continue...** (shown in the preceding screenshot) to start the synchronization, as shown in the following screenshot:

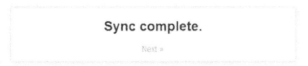

Depending on how many users and groups will be synchronized, this can take from a few seconds to a few hours.

Once completed, click on **Next >>** to continue. You will now see the **Select Modules** screen, as shown in the following screenshot:

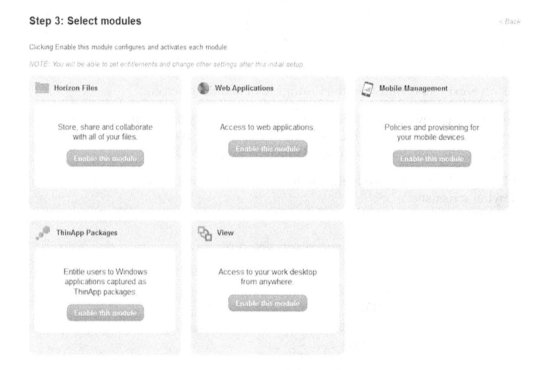

On this screen, you would click on the green **Enable this module** button to enable each module. A module is a particular feature/function that Horizon Workspace delivers. We will leave these for now and enable them in the chapters that cover that particular feature.

Click on the green **Next >** button to continue to the next stage, as shown in the following screenshot:

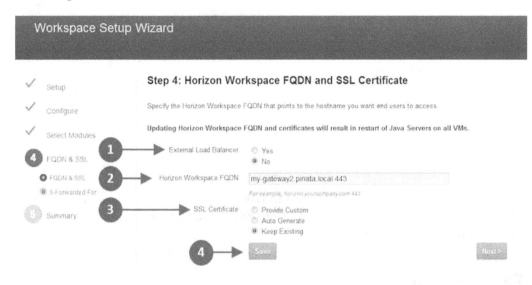

On the FQDN and SSL Certificate screen, first click on the radio button depending on if you have an external load balancer (**1**). Then enter the FQDN for your Horizon Workspace (**2**), and finally click on the radio button for selecting the type of SSL certificate (**3**).

 If this is a POC environment, then it is recommended that you keep the existing certificates to reduce complexity during setup.

Click on **Save** (**4**) once you have entered the information, and then click on **Next >**.

You will now see the **X-Forwarded-For** screen. The **X-Forwarded-For** screen allows Horizon Workspace to extract the original IP address of your users, rather than seeing all the sessions coming from the load balancer.

If you have a reverse proxy or a load balancer in front of Horizon Workspace and want to use it, then enter the IP address of the sender here.

Click on **Save** once you have entered the information and then click on **Next >**.

The final screen you will see is the **Summary** screen, as shown in the following screenshot:

To complete the installation, click on **Go to Horizon Workspace >**. You will now be taken to the configuration page where you can start enabling and configuring the different Horizon Workspace modules.

Summary

In this chapter, we have covered the deployment of Horizon Workspace, starting with the vApp, the initial configuration steps using the command line and console, and then finally the browser-based Setup Wizard to set up and synchronize information about the users and the groups from the Active Directory.

In the following chapters, we will look at the Horizon Workspace modules in more detail, starting with Horizon Files in the next chapter.

3
Horizon Files

Horizon Workspace is a platform that integrates a number of different components to deliver a complete workspace to an end user. It has the ability to deliver files, applications, and desktop and mobile applications to an end user on the device that they choose based on a corporate policy. In this chapter, we will discuss Horizon Workspace's file and data collaboration features and functionalities — Horizon Workspace Files and how to configure and manage it.

An introduction to Horizon Workspace Files

Horizon Files was first introduced as a tech preview at VMworld 2011 under the code name of Project Octopus. It was then released as part of Horizon Workspace 1.0.

So, what is Horizon Files? Horizon Files is an on-premise file collaboration platform that allows users to share files both internally and externally; however, the key thing to remember here is that the data is secure as it is actually hosted on your corporately owned internal infrastructure rather than in a cloud-based service. This gives the IT department control over the data, and more importantly cover how the information is shared.

As we will discuss in this chapter, your files can be accessed using native applications from many different devices, such as Windows desktops and laptops, Macintosh, iOS, and Android devices. You can also use a web browser from any device if no native application is available.

Whichever device you use, your data will be consistent across any and all of your devices as will the look and feel of the user interface.

Horizon data appliance architecture

Before we get into the configuration, we are going to take a high-level look at the Horizon Files element of the workspace architecture and the virtual appliances that power it. These are shown in the following figure:

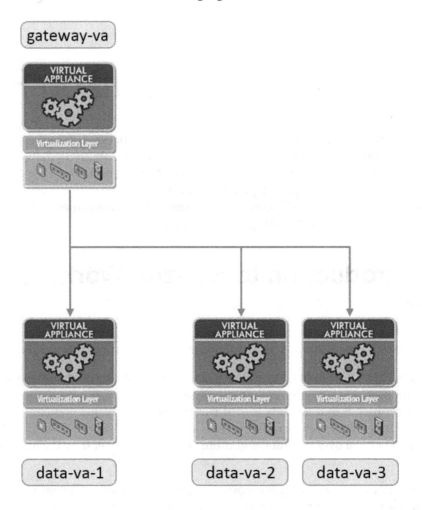

The deployment in the preceding figure is based on the minimum requirements for a production deployment that requires a recommended minimum of three data appliances.

The first data-va virtual machine that gets deployed is a master data node and should not contain user data. The master data node contains the user LDAP database. Additional nodes are used for user data, with each node being capable of supporting up to 1,000 users.

A dedicated storage volume is required by each node and is dependent on the type of deployment. In a POC or small-scale pilot, or when the storage requirement is less than 6 GB, you can use a **VMware Virtual Machine Disk (VMDK)**, but for a production environment, you should follow the VMware recommendation and use an NFS-based storage. The reason for using NFS is due to VMFS5 being limited to a maximum of 25 TB of virtual disks open per host. They would also need to be divided into 2 TB chunks with the heap size needing to be set to 8 MB to support that. This would limit the number of users per host.

Configuring storage on the data-va virtual machine

When we deployed the data-va virtual machine, it was automatically configured with several VMDK files totaling 175 GB. However, only one of these files is configured to store Horizon Files blobs (user data) and by default is only 10 GB in size.

So the first thing we need to do is to add some additional disk space so that we can manage our Horizon Files storage resources and user requirements.

Calculating user storage requirements

Before adding additional storage it is probably a good idea to work out how much storage you will need. The total will be governed by the size of the quota you allow each user. As a rule of thumb, the total for each user should be two and a half times their quota. That would allow users to store two revisions of any document. For each additional document revision you want to allow them to store, you need to add and additional 0.5 x quota.

Adding a new VMDK

To add a new VMDK to the data-va appliance, the first thing we need to do is to actually create a new VMDK in vSphere. Once you have added a new VMDK, then you will need to reboot the data-va virtual machine.

Once rebooted, we now need to add the storage to the data-va appliance. Log in to the console of the data-va appliance as root using the password created during the initial installation. On the command line, run the following command:

```
/opt/vmware-hdva-installer/bin/zca-expand-lv
```

The appliance will now detect the new disk and add it to the logical store volume and you can then log out of the console.

Adding a new NFS data store

As we did in the previous section, the first thing to do is to create a new NFS share and make a note of the hostname and the directory you want to mount. Ensure that the data-va appliance can access the NFS server.

Log in to the console of the data-va appliance as root using the password created during the initial installation. On the command line, run the following command:

```
/opt/vmware-hdva-installer/bin # ./mount-nfs-store.pl --nfsnfs_server:/
directory
```

You should now have a new volume to use for storing user files.

Enabling Horizon Files and entitling users

In the installation section of this chapter, we installed and configured the virtual appliances for Horizon Workspace. Before we can start using any of the features, we need to enable them. In the following section, we will enable the Horizon Files module.

Enabling the Horizon Files module

First, we need to access the Horizon Workspace admin portal, so open a browser and go to the following address `https://FQDN_to_Workspace/Admin`. In this example, the address would be `https://my-gateway2.pinata.local/Admin`.

Enable the module named **Horizon Files** by clicking on the green **Enable this module** button (1). This is shown in the following screenshot:

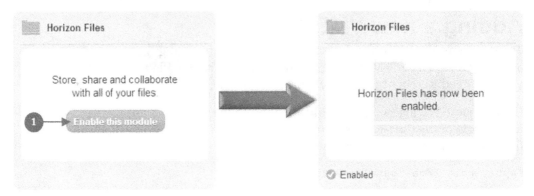

Even though we have enabled the **Horizon Files** module, users will still not have access to it. So, the next step is to create some user entitlements that will allow users to make use of the features of Horizon Files.

Entitling users to Horizon Files

Now that we have enabled the Horizon Files modules, we need to allow users to access it. To do this, we need to be logged in to the admin portal and perform the following steps:

1. From the menu tabs across the top of the screen, click on **Catalog (1)**, as shown in the following screenshot:

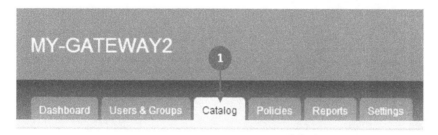

2. Now click on **Services (2)**, as shown in the following screenshot:

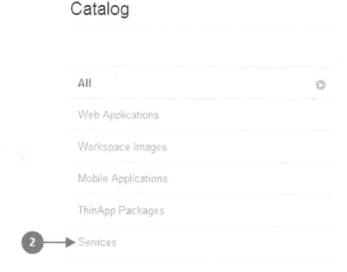

3. Finally, click on the **Horizon Files** folder icon (**3**), as shown in the following screenshot:

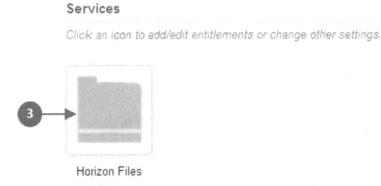

You should now see the following screen:

From here we can entitle groups or individual users to the Horizon Files service. The users and groups information is synchronized from Active Directory. You can also see the ID of the Horizon Files service and also the ability to configure the **Class of Service** (**COS**), which we will cover in the following section.

We are now going to entitle a user, so click on the **+ Add a new User Entitlement** button. You will see a dialog box, as shown in the following screenshot:

In our example, we will entitle **Test User2** to the Horizon Files service, so in the textbox, start typing the name of the user. It will filter results as you type.

As you can see, we only got as far as typing `test`.

Click on **User2, Test (testuser2)**. This user will now appear in the dialog box, as shown in the following screenshot:

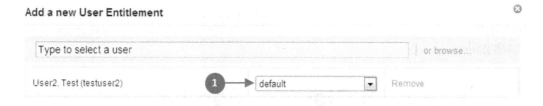

In this dialog box, you can also select the COS that would apply to this user by clicking on the drop-down menu (**1**). As we haven't yet configured any COS settings, we will leave this as **default**. Click on the green **Save** button in the right-hand corner of the page.

A COS is a user policy that defines how they are allowed to share files internally and externally and also the amount of storage space allocated to them. A user can have only one COS assigned to them at one time. We will discuss the COS options in the *Configuring a Class of Service* section.

You will return to the main entitlement screen and the following message will be displayed:

New actions are disabled until you are finished with entitlements. Click the Done button to update the tables. Existing accounts will continue to work while entitlements are modified.

Done

As we are only going to entitle one user, click on the **Done** button to update the tables. If you were adding additional users, you would continue to do this, and click on **Done** when completed. You will now see that the user has been entitled to use Horizon Files, as shown in the following screenshot:

User Entitlements (1)   ✚ Add a new User Entitlement

USER	ACTIVE COS	PROVISIONING STATUS
User2, Test (testuser2)	default	Unentitle

Now, the user has been entitled to Horizon Files. In the following section, we will look at how we configure what they can and can't do in terms of uploading and sharing files.

Configuring a Class of Service

Horizon Files uses a COS to define a policy around what a user is allowed to do. In this example, we are going to take a look at the default COS policy and the options that are available to configure in building our own COS. A COS can apply to either a user or a group, but a user/group can only have one COS applied to them at any time.

To configure a COS, click on the **Class of Service (1)** option in the entitlements screen.

You will then see the following screenshot which displays the current valid COS configurations. From here you can view, edit, copy, or create a new COS.

In this example, we are going to view the default COS and look at the configurations; so click on **default** (**2**) to view the default COS.

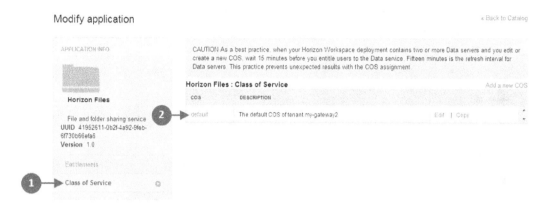

You will now see the default COS displayed.

> If you have more than one data-va appliance, any changes or new COS that you create will take 15 minutes before it will be applied to the users as this is the refresh interval between the virtual appliances.

COS configuration options

We are now going to take a look at the options that you can configure as part of the COS. We will break these down into sections. The first of these is shown in the following screenshot:

In this first section, you simply give your COS a name (**1**) and then a meaningful description (**2**).

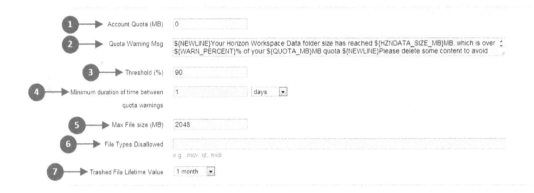

In the section shown in the previous screenshot, you have the following options:

- **Account Quota (MB)** (**1**): Here you can enter the size of the storage allocated for this COS.

- **Quota Warning Msg** (**2**): Here you can enter the message that a user will see when they get to a certain percentage of their allocated quota. A quota in this context is the amount of storage space a user has been allocated.

- **Threshold (%)** (**3**): Here you can enter the threshold where the quota warnings should start to generate.

- **Minimum duration of time between quota warnings** (**4**): Here you can set how often a user will see the warning messages. The drop-down box allows you to change the duration to days, hours, minutes, and seconds.

- **Max File size (MB)** (**5**): Here you can set the maximum file size a user can upload.

- **File Types Disallowed** (**6**): Here you can block users from uploading particular file types. These are entered by the extension type. For example, .mp3, .avi, and so on.

- **Trashed File Lifetime Value** (**7**): Here you can set how long a deleted file remains in the trash where a user can undelete it. The drop-down box allows you to configure the months, for example, 1, 3, 6, and 12 months.

These options are all based on what the user can do internally and also the management of their files' account.

The next section, displayed in the following screenshot, shows the configurable options on how users can share files both internally and externally:

In the section shown in the previous screenshot, you have the following options for configuring how a user shares files:

- **Internal Expiration (1)**: Here you can configure a time limit on how long a shared file or folder lives for. The dropdown allows you to configure days, hours, minutes, and seconds.

- **External Folder Sharing Allowed (2)**: Tick this box to allow a user to share a folder with external people.

- **Public Files Sharing Allowed (3)**: Tick this box to allow a user to share an individual file with external people.

- **External Expiration (4)**: Here you can configure a time limit on how long an externally shared folder lives for. The dropdown allows you to configure days, hours, minutes, and seconds.

- **Public Expiration (5)**: Here you can configure a time limit on how long an externally shared file lives for. The dropdown allows you to configure days, hours, minutes, and seconds.

- **Domains Allowed or Not Allowed (6)**: Here you have the following three options represented by the radio buttons:

    ○ **No Domain Policy**: This allows users to share files and folders with anybody internally or externally

- ○ **Allowed**: This allows you to specify which domain names are allowed
- ○ **Restricted**: This allows you to specify which domain names are not allowed to stop users sending to potentially unsafe external people

The last section shows the data hosts that are in the pool and a couple of mobile options. These options are shown in the following screenshot:

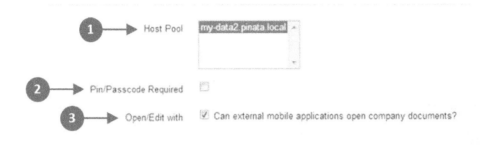

The following is the description of the options shown in the previous screenshot:

- **Host Pool (1)**: This displays the data-va servers in the pool
- **Pin/Passcode Required (2)**: Tick this box if you want the user to access the Horizon Files App using a pin code
- **Open/Edit with (3)**: Ticking this box allows users to open documents with external applications that the user already has on their device rather than only with apps securely delivered via their workspace

Return to the main dashboard page by clicking on the **Dashboard** tab.

User accounts

Horizon Files uses two types of user accounts to allow users access their files.

Domain users

The obvious type of user account is the Domain account used by all internal employees to access the network and their workspace. This is just a user's standard AD account, username, and password. Horizon Workspace reads the user information from AD.

Virtual users

Specific to Horizon Files, a virtual user gets created when you share a folder with an external e-mail address. The person you invite will be sent a URL that directs them to a Horizon Workspace page where they can set up their own virtual user account by creating a password. Their username will be the e-mail address that you used to send the URL. They then have the same look and feel of Horizon Workspace as any other user but just containing the folders that you have shared with them. They will also be limited to using just the web-browser interface and not the native Horizon application. We will cover this in more detail in the *Sharing a file* section of this chapter.

Document preview

One of the features of Horizon Files is the ability to preview documents within the browser of your device without actually opening the document.

This is particularly useful when using a device such as an iPad, as it allows you to preview Microsoft Office documents. There are two options for previewing files.

LibreOffice

You will find an installer script on the data-va appliance, ready built for the install and download of LibreOffice.

 The data-va appliance will need to have an Internet access as the LibreOffice files are going to be automatically downloaded.

Perform the following steps to complete the installation:

1. From your vSphere client, open a console window to your data-va appliance.
2. Log in as the root user with the password you used in the deployment of the vApp.
3. On the command line, run the following command:

   `/opt/zimbra/libexec/libreoffice-installer.sh`

4. Once the installation has completed, you need to restart the data-va service using the Zimbra user by running the following commands:

   `su zimbra`

   `zmmailboxdctl restart`

If you don't have access to the Internet from your data appliance, there is a way to install LibreOffice manually. Firstly, you need to go to the LibreOffice website and download the installation package from `http://tinyurl.com/q8rpndq`.

Once downloaded, you need to copy it onto a local web server or somewhere else internally that the data-va appliance has access to.

You will also need to modify the installer script so as to point it to the local location. When you edit the script, update `LIBREOFFICE_URL=http://<server address>`, where `<server address>` is the location of the downloaded package.

Microsoft Windows Preview

Instead of LibreOffice, you could use Microsoft Windows Preview. However, you still need to install LibreOffice as well. The other point to note is that there could be additional license cost implications in deploying the Microsoft solution, whereas LibreOffice is licensed under the terms of the LGPLv3 and is free for personal and commercial use. Microsoft Preview will render MS Office documents with a better accuracy than LibreOffice.

There are two steps to the installation process: installing Microsoft Windows Preview being the first step and then linking it to your data-va appliance as the second step.

To install Microsoft Windows Preview, first ensure that you have LibreOffice installed and are using either Windows 7 Enterprise Edition or Windows Server 2008 R2 Standard as the platform to run from. Typically, a server OS would be used for this.

 The recommended sizing for Microsoft Windows Preview is a virtual machine configured with 8 vCPU, 4 GB RAM, and 32 GB hard disk. This will service approximately 1000 users.

To start the installation process, first download the `.msi` file from the following Horizon Workspace download directory: `/opt/zimbra/jetty/webapps/zimbra/downloads/VMware-Horizon-Data-Preview-Server-buildnumber.msi`.

Accept the **End-user license agreement (EULA)** and click on **Next** until you are prompted for the controller/worker password. The password is `VMware123!`. If prompted, reboot the server.

 The controller account is logged in automatically after the reboot and must be logged in for the server to run.

The next step in the process is to point the data-va appliance to the Preview Server. Log in to the console of the data-va appliance as root using the password created during the initial installation. On the command line, run the following command to change to the Zimbra user:

```
su - zimbra
```

To point the data-va appliance at the Windows Preview Server, type the following command on the command line:

```
zmlocalconfig -e ms_converter_url= http://preview.server.address
```

Once completed, you need to restart the service by entering the following command on the command line:

```
Zmmailboxdctl
```

The final step in the process is to modify each of the COS configurations to ensure they are using the correct preview mechanism. To do this, use the following command, replacing <cosname> with the name of each COS you have configured:

```
zmprov mc <cosname> hzndataConverterHints UseMsPDFConverter
```

Managing files and folders

In this section, we are going to take a closer look at Horizon Files from a user's perspective and how they would use its features and functionalities.

First of all, let's log in as a user. To do this, go to the URL of the workspace; in our sample lab, it's https://my-gateway2.pinata.local. We will log in as testuser2, as shown in the following screenshot:

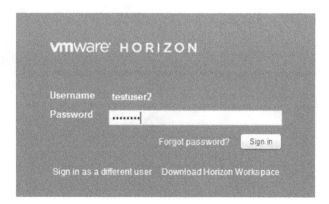

Once logged in, we will see our workspace and by default, the first thing we see is the **Files** tab, as shown in the following screenshot:

One of the admin features of Horizon Files allows the IT department to upload and prepopulate content. This means they could upload things such as company handbooks and policy documents, for example, which mean everyone gets them by default.

To prepopulate content, copy the files to the following directory on the data-va: `/opt/zimbra/jetty-distribution-7.6.2.z4/static/`.

Uploading a file

As this is the first time this particular user has logged in, they currently do not have any files uploaded. The next step is to upload files. As an example, we have created a text file using WordPad and saved it locally in `My Documents`.

To upload a file, click on the drop-down arrow (**1**) and then click on **Upload** (**2**), as shown in the following screenshot. You could also drag-and-drop files into the file list.

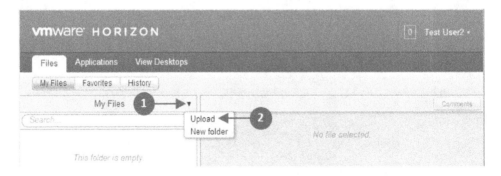

A dialog box opens that allows you to browse and select a file. Select the example file we created. It will now appear in the **My Files** pane on the left-hand side, as shown in the following screenshot:

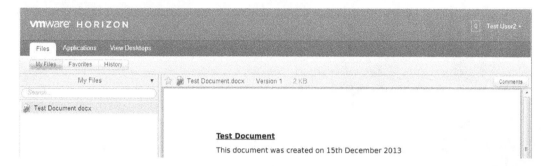

If you now click on the document we just uploaded it will be displayed in the preview pane to the right of the **My Files** pane. You also have a number of other options shown at the bottom of that screen (shown in the following screenshot), which we will quickly describe:

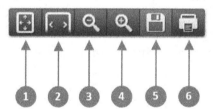

The following is the description of the previously described options:

- **1**: View the document as a whole page
- **2**: View the document the full width of the screen
- **3**: Zoom out
- **4**: Zoom in
- **5**: Save
- **6**: Print

You also have a number of options available by highlighting a specific file and clicking on the down arrow. These are shown in the following screenshot:

The following is the description of the options in the previous screenshot:

- **Share Publicly (1)**: This opens a dialog box containing a link that you can send to external users (policy dependent) in order to share an individual file.
- **Favorite (2)**: This adds the present document to your **Favorites** tab, which also allows offline access on devices such as iPads. Only files marked as **Favorite** are available offline on mobile devices such as Android and iPads.
- **History (3)**: This shows the history of the present document.
- **Download (4)**: This downloads a copy to the local device (policy dependent).
- **Rename (5)**: This allows you to rename the file.
- **Move (6)**: This allows you to move the file to another folder.
- **Delete (7)**: This deletes the file.

Sharing a file

As an example, we will share the file we just uploaded in the previous section.

To share a file, you first need to highlight the file you want to share and right-click on it. From the menu options shown in the previous screenshot, click on **Share Publicly** (**1**). It's then just a case of copying the link and e-mailing it.

Version control

Another feature of Horizon Files is the ability to track updates to document versions. This allows users to collaborate on documents, showing the latest version and also the ability to roll back to the previous version.

In our example, we are going to open the WordPad document we created and uploaded earlier, make some changes, save it, and then upload it again. If you had the Horizon Agent installed and opened the document from the Horizon folder, you would not need to manually upload the document as it will synchronize automatically. This will be covered later in this chapter.

The current version of the document is shown at the top of the preview pane, as shown in the following screenshot. If you click on the down arrow (**1**), all the versions will be displayed.

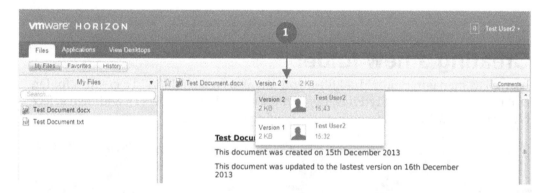

Clicking on an older version will give you three options, as shown in the following screenshot, to show the latest versions; make the currently selected documents the latest or download it:

Comments

As you collaborate on a document with a colleague, a useful feature is the comment feature. This allows you to add comments to a document that will be viewed by all those that are sharing the document. The **Comments** button can be found on the right-hand side along the top of the preview pane. Clicking on it opens a new pane allowing you to add comments.

To add a comment, first type your text in the box (**1**) and then click on **Add Comment** (**2**). This is shown in the following screenshot:

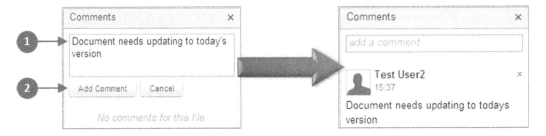

Creating a new folder

As well as managing individual files, you can also create folders. To create a folder, make sure you click on **My Files**, then on the drop-down arrow (**1**), and then select **New Folder** (**2**). This is shown in the following screenshot:

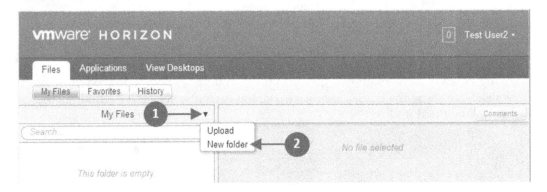

A new folder appears on the left-hand side, as shown in the following screenshot. Type in a name for the new folder as shown in the following screenshot:

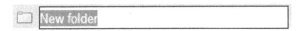

Sharing a folder

You can also share a folder with other internal or external users. In this example, we will share the folder we created in the previous step. To do this, highlight the folder you want to share and click on the down arrow (1). Click on **Share** (2), as shown in the following screenshot:

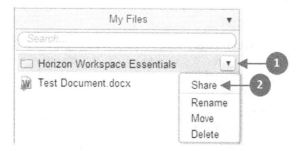

A dialog box will now be shown where you can enter the details of the e-mail address of the person you want to share the folder with. There are three options: **view**, **view and edit**, and **view, edit and share**, as shown in the following screenshot:

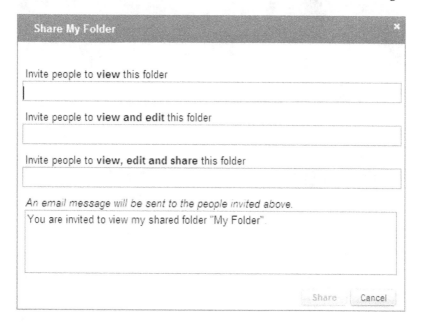

Once you have entered the e-mail addresses for the level of access you want the external user to have, click on **Share**. This will also be based on the policy of what domain names are allowed or not allowed to share information with; otherwise, you could see the following message:

⚠ External accounts are not allowed to "view, edit and share".

 One of the prerequisites for Horizon Workspace is to have an SMTP service running. This feature is the reason why you need to have it—to allow you to send the external sharing requests to the user's e-mail address.

In our example, we are going to share a folder with an external user and then look at the experience from their perspective and what exactly they will see.

The first thing they will see is the e-mail notification with a link for them to follow. An example is shown in the following screenshot:

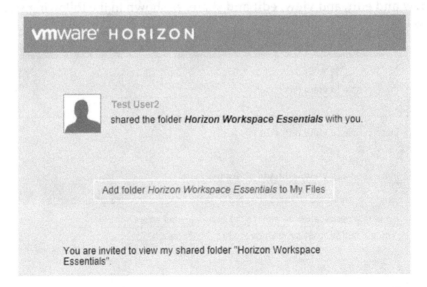

Click on the **Add folder Horizon Workspace Essentials to My Files** link. If this is the first time that you have shared a folder with this user, then the first thing they are asked for when clicking on the link is to create a virtual user account for themselves. This is shown in the following screenshot:

Once the user has created their virtual user account, any subsequent folders that are shared will mean that they will automatically appear in the user's account within their Workspace Files (**1**), as shown in the following screenshot. From here, they can click on **Add to My Files**, that is, accept the share, or click on **Ignore** to discard it. They will also be sent an e-mail.

History

The last part of Horizon Files we are going to cover is the **History** tab. If you click on the **History** tab (**1**), you will see the following screen:

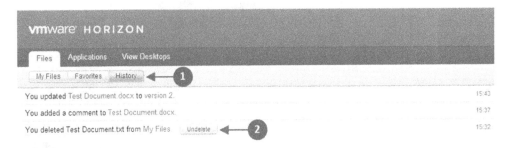

From this view, you can see an overview of all the file's activity on your account, from uploading documents to leaving comments. Probably the most important thing is the **Undelete** button (**2**). This allows you to restore a deleted file. Bear in mind that the length of time a file remains restorable depends on the policy set in the user's COS.

Synchronizing Horizon Files and offline access

Everything we have discussed so far has been based on the user being online. In this section, we are going to cover how a user can continue to have access to their files while being disconnected or offline.

Having the Horizon Workspace Agent installed on your endpoint device enables this feature. The Horizon Agent is available for Microsoft Windows and Apple Mac OS X.

The agent can be downloaded by clicking on the down arrow next to the username (**1**) and then clicking on **Download Horizon** (**2**), as shown in the following screenshot:

The download link will direct you to the appropriate operating system depending on the device from which you are currently accessing your Horizon Workspace. In this case, it will direct us to the Windows download.

The next step is to install the agent. We are going to do this manually by performing the following steps, but you could include this as part of a desktop build:

1. Run the Horizon Workspace Agent installer: `VMware-Horizon-Workspace-1.5.2-1439142.exe`.

2. Click on **Next>** to accept the VMware EULA.

3. Click on **Next>** to accept the default installation folder.

4. Type in the name of your Horizon Server and click on **OK**.

The installation is now complete and you will see the Horizon Workspace icon on the task bar, as shown in the following screenshot:

To link your machine to your Horizon Workspace account and allow the synchronization, you will need to log in. To do this, perform the following steps:

1. Right-click on the Horizon Workspace cloud icon on the task bar.

2. Click on **Sign into Horizon Workspace**.

3. Enter your username and password.

Your Horizon Workspace is now connected to your account, as you can see in the following screenshot:

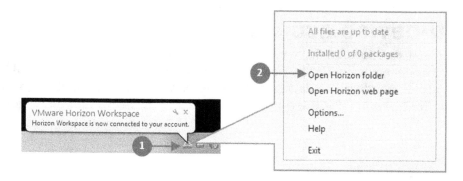

Along with connecting your account, the agent install will have also created a local `Horizon` folder in Windows Explorer (or Finder if you use a Mac).

Right-click on the Horizon Workspace icon (**1**) and then click on **Open Horizon folder** (**2**). A Windows Explorer window should now open. Browse the `Horizon` folder and compare its contents with those shown within your **Files** view in the online version.

Depending on the size of the files, you should now see that the two are synchronized, as shown in the following screenshot:

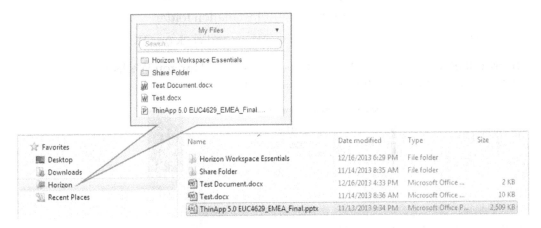

Having this capability allows a user to work on their files offline. When they reconnect, anything they have worked on offline that gets saved in the `Horizon` folder will be synchronized.

The process for downloading the Workspace agent for Mac OS X is similar to how we have previously described it for Windows devices, with the agent available in the same way. You would then just follow the usual application installation process you would use on a Mac.

Multi-device access

In the previous sections, we have predominantly talked about the Windows operating system; however, the whole ethos behind Horizon Workspace is to allow users to access their files and data from any device, while maintaining the same user interface. For Horizon Files, there are also apps for both iOS and Android devices.

The Android app

The following screenshot shows a user logged into Horizon Files using an Android smartphone. As you can see, they get a view of exactly the same files as they did when using a Windows PC or an Apple Mac.

The user is also able to preview their files.

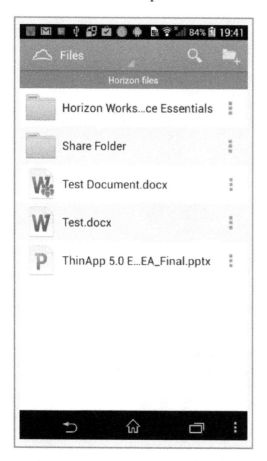

The iOS app

The following screenshot shows a user logged into Horizon Files using an iPad:

Again, you can see that they get a view of exactly the same files as they did when using a Windows PC, Apple Mac, or an Android device, along with the ability to preview files.

Summary

In this chapter, we have covered an introduction into Horizon Files, firstly from the IT administrator's perspective, demonstrating how to enable, configure, and entitle users. We then covered the user's aspect on how to use Horizon Files to share, upload, and manage their files and data from multiple devices.

In the next chapter, we will discuss the process for integrating **Software as a Service (SaaS)** applications and using Horizon Workspace for authentication to cloud-based services.

Integrating SaaS Applications

In this chapter, we will have a look at how we broker to web-based applications in VMware Horizon Workspace 1.5.

One of the core features of Horizon Workspace is the ability to entitle and consume web-based applications, also known as **Software-as-a-Service (SaaS)**.

It's a clear trend that many companies use SaaS applications that are provided by an external partner, such as Google, Salesforce, and Microsoft.

Once you start to use these services, it often becomes complex for the users and IT to set up and administer them, since they all have separate user management, password policies, and so on.

A solution to this complexity is Identity Federation, the idea being to use your corporate identity such as your **Active Directory (AD)** identity and extend it to the external service to reduce this complexity and enhance the user experience.

The most common way of doing this is to use a standard-based solution called **Security Assertion Markup Language (SAML)**. It's an XML protocol that is designed to transfer authentication and authorization information between different systems.

SAML is not only used for SaaS, but can also be used to integrate to other services, for example, VMware View. We will see more about that in *Chapter 7, Horizon View Integration*.

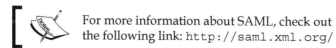

For more information about SAML, check out the following link: `http://saml.xml.org/`

Horizon Workspace 1.5 is compatible with SAML 1.1 and 2.0 federation standards.

Configuring SAML-based SaaS apps

When configuring a web-based application, you first need to configure a trust between your Horizon Workspace instance and the application provider.

When the user launches the application, a SAML assertion is created and is valid for 30 seconds. The 30 seconds is also referred to as the **Time to Live (TTL)**. The generated assertion is posted into the web-based service using the URI browser string in the end user's browser. The service will decode the SAML assertion, verify that it's valid, verify the certificate, and then authenticate the user.

The user does not need to enter a username or password, as they are simply authenticated automatically to the web application.

There are different levels of SAML integration as follows:

- **Single Sign-On (SSO)**: SSO using the existing AD credentials
- **Provisioning**: Automatic creation and deletion of users

In this example, we will set up an SSO connection to Salesforce from Horizon Workspace. The process will be different, depending on the web-based application that you want to integrate to, but it should follow the same principle.

Configuring Horizon Workspace for SaaS apps

Start by logging in to the Horizon Workspace portal with the admin account. On the dashboard, enable the **Web Applications** module by clicking on the green **Enable this module** button (1), as shown in the following screenshot:

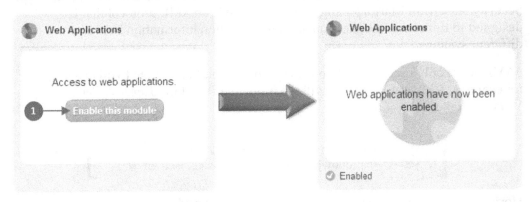

Now, we have enabled the **Web Applications** module. The next step is to configure some SaaS applications and then entitle users to the applications using the following steps:

1. From the menu tabs at the top of the screen, click on **Catalog (1)**, as shown in the following screenshot:

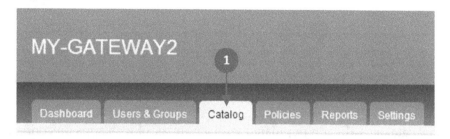

2. Now click on **Web Applications (2)**, as shown in the following screenshot:

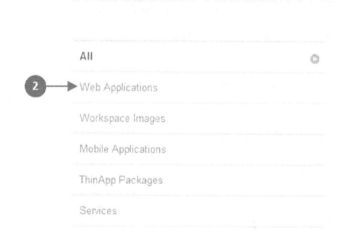

3. Click on the **+ Web Application** button (**3**) on the right-hand side of the screen and select the option **...from your Global Catalog** (**4**), as shown in the following screenshot:

The global catalog is already populated with a number of web apps preconfigured to make it much easier to set up the integration. If your application is not in the global catalog, you need to set up the integration using the **...create a new one** option.

This option requires more detailed knowledge about the integration configuration and the remote system. The already listed integrations are much simpler to set up since most of the details have been preconfigured for you.

In this sample scenario, we will use Salesforce. This is a supported integration and appears in the global catalog.

You should now see the global catalog as shown in the following screenshot.

Locate **Salesforce** (**1**) in the global catalog and click on it.

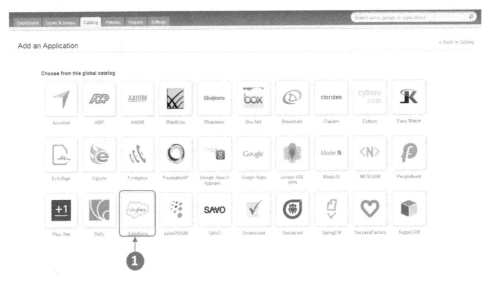

You will now see the following screenshot:

Enter a suitable name (**1**) and a description (**2**). You also have the option to choose your own icon by clicking on **Choose File** (**3**). Once completed, click on **Save** (**4**).

We will need to entitle a user or a group to be able to use the application. In this example, we will use TestUser2 to entitle to this application.

You should now see the entitlement screen, as shown in the following screenshot:

Now click on **+ Add user entitlement (1)**.

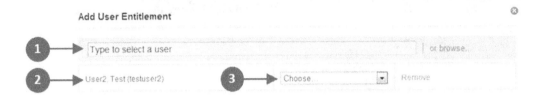

As shown in the previous screenshot, type the name of the user (**1**). The user needs to be one who is synchronized with Horizon Workspace from the AD. Once found, add the user (**2**).

From the drop-down box (**3**), you need to choose a deployment method. There are two types of deployment, which are as follows:

- **User Activated**: The user needs to activate the application manually from the application catalog
- **Automatic**: The application will be added to the user's main Workspace screen without the need for any user action

Once the details have been completed, click on the green **Save** button, and you will get the following screenshot.

Verify that the users and the groups are correct. In the next section, we will configure the SaaS provider's application for Horizon Workspace.

Configuring the SaaS app for Horizon Workspace

We have completed the Horizon Workspace part of the configuration. We now need to set up the integration on the Salesforce side.

Before we do that, we need to first save the SAML Certificate from Horizon Workspace to a file.

Navigate to the **Settings** tab (**1**) and then click on **SAML Certificate** (**2**). Block all the text in the **Signing Certificate** field (**3**), right-click on the text, and choose **Copy**. Open a text editor and paste the content into it. Save the file with a `.cer` file extension, for example, `saml.cer`, as shown in the following screenshot:

Now we need to complete the setup on the Salesforce side. If you have not done so previously, you need to create a developer account on `http://developerforce.com`.

 The Salesforce developer account is free of charge, but has restrictions on the number of users and the amount of data used.

Once you have created an account and logged in, you will be presented with the administration interface, as shown in the following screenshot:

Click on **Security Controls (1)** on the left-hand side menu and then select **Single Sign-On Settings (2)**. Click on **Edit (3)** to get the option to enable SAML. You will see the following screenshot:

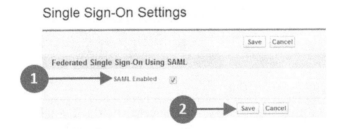

Check the **SAML Enabled** box **(1)** and then click on **Save (2)**.

You will now see the following screenshot:

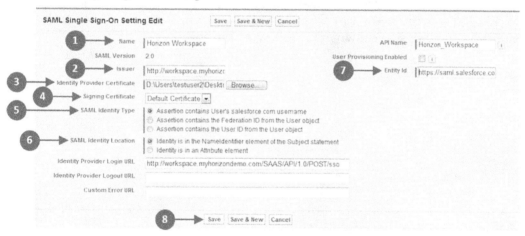

Click on **New (1)** to start setting up the configuration details.

You will now see the editing screen for SAML SSO, as shown in the following screenshot:

Now you need to fill in the following details of your Horizon Workspace implementation:

- **Name (1)**: You can choose an appropriate name

- **Issuer (2)**: This should be the FQDN to your Workspace implementation; add `/SAAS/API/1.0/GET/metadata.idp.xml`

- **Identity Provider Certificate (3)**: Upload the file that you saved earlier with the `.cer` extension

- **Signing Certificate (4)**: Leave this as default

- **SAML Identity Type (5)**: Leave this as default
- **Identity Provider Login URL (6)**: This should be the FQDN to your Workspace implementation; add `/SAAS/API/1.0/POST/sso`
- **Entity Id (7)**: This should be `https://saml.salesforce.com`

Once you have filled in the values, click on **Save (8)** to save the new settings. The result should be something similar to the following screenshot:

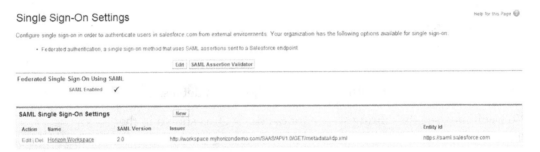

If something is not correct or you need to make a change later, simply click on **Edit** to change the settings. You can use the **SAML Assertion Validator** button (**1**) to validate the settings, as shown in the following screenshot:

Next, we need to create a user. From the left-hand side menu, click on **Manage Users** (**1**), **Users** (**2**), and then **New User** (**3**), as shown in the following screenshot:

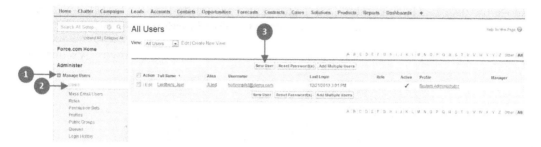

Fill in the information for the user as shown in the following screenshot.

> It's important that the **Email** field (the login) matches the information in your Horizon Workspace environment.

A password is not needed, as the user will not need any password to log in.

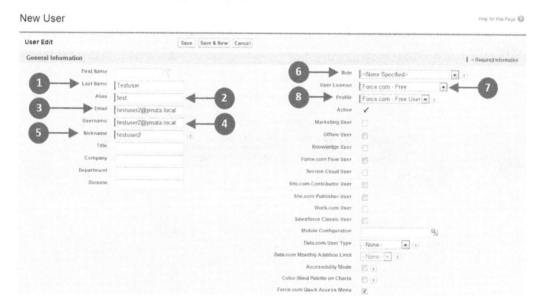

In our example, we will use the TestUser2 account. Enter the **Last Name** (**1**), the user **Alias** (**2**), the user's **Email** (**3**), the **Username** as it appears in the AD (**4**), and a **Nickname** for the user (**5**).

Finally, leave the **Role** field as **<None Specified>** (6), set the **User License** to **Force. com – Free** (7), and the **Profile** to **Force.com – Free User** (8).

Once the user has been created in Salesforce and assuming that the SAML settings are correct, we should be able to test whether the SSO functionality works.

Log in to Horizon Workspace using `testuser2`, as shown in the following screenshot:

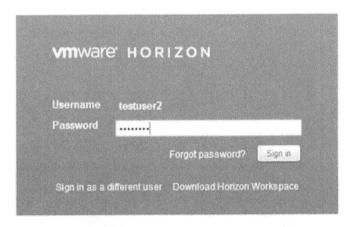

Once logged in, you will see the Workspace for testuser2, as shown in the following screenshot:

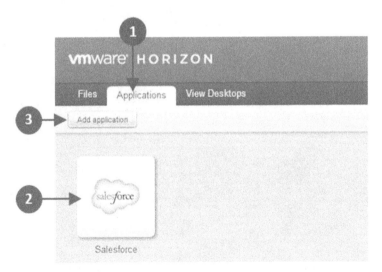

Click on the **Applications** tab (**1**).

If we chose **Automatic** as the deployment method, then **Salesforce** (**2**) should be visible on the **Applications** tab of the user's Workspace when we log in.

If the deployment method chosen was **User Activated**, then you will need to click on **Add application** (3) and add the Salesforce application from the catalog.

Now click on the Salesforce icon. The browser will open a new window or browser tab and post the SAML assertion into the browser window (notice the long text string in the URI field shown in the following screenshot). In a few seconds, the user will be logged in to Salesforce.

Notice that you did not need to type in a username or password to access Salesforce, yet the username states that you are logged in as testuser2.

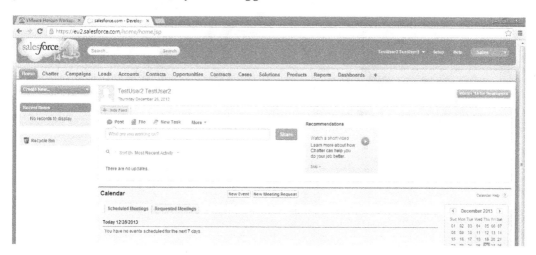

Summary

In this chapter, we discussed web-based applications and how they can be integrated with Horizon Workspace. We discussed SAML assertions as a way of securely extending your corporate identity to other systems, namely third-party SaaS providers.

Finally, we also took you through the step-by-step process of how to configure integration with Salesforce.

In the next chapter, we will discuss Mobile Management with Horizon Workspace.

5
Mobile Management

In this chapter, we will discuss the mobile management capabilities of VMware Horizon Workspace 1.5, including configuration, device enrollment, and how to entitle users to mobile applications.

An overview of Horizon Workspace on a mobile

Mobile management has become a hot topic on every IT department's agenda. Historically, Microsoft ActiveSync and Blackberry were the two main mobile phone management solutions. With the release of Apple's iPhone and Google's Android, it has become clear that we need another way to manage our corporate data that is stored on mobile devices. **Enterprise Mobile Management** (**EMM**) is still very much an emerging technology, and many startup companies have jumped into this market space with a wide range of solutions, all with different capabilities.

The mobile market of today is dominated by two mobile operating systems: Apple's iOS and Google's Android. Android is the fastest growing platform, but iOS has a stable market share, especially in the USA and European markets. Other types of devices such as Windows Mobile or Blackberry have a limited market share when compared to Apple and Android. In comparison, the challenges that a company faces in supporting iOS and Android couldn't be more different.

Apple has a very strict and controlled environment. Applications (apps) must go through Apple's control before they get published on the Apple App Store, and the devices pretty much act and support the same features. Google, on the other hand, is the opposite. Anyone can more or less build and sell an Android device and Google does not actively govern the published apps on the Google Play Store.

The diversity of the Android platform is the reason many companies decided not to support it. It's simply too hard to keep up with the different Android versions and device capabilities. VMware Horizon Workspace takes a truly unique approach to solve the diversity of the Android's platform. Horizon Workspace creates a virtual Android image running on top of the native Android operating system on the device. This is very much like other VMware products such as VMware Workstation, where you run a virtual operating systems on top of a Windows operating system. This way IT departments can focus on managing one image that is the same, irrespective of the device on which it's running on, and all corporate data is kept in a secure virtualized container.

Horizon Workspace's virtual Android supports dual data plans on one **Subscriber Identity Module (SIM)**. So if the carrier supports dual data plans on one SIM, your private Android can have your private phone number and data plan while your virtual corporate Android image can have a separate corporate phone number and data plan. If your carrier does not support dual data plans on one SIM, you can still use the virtual Android on your device. Both phones will then use the same phone number and data plan.

There is one limitation with VMware's solution. In order to be able to run the virtual Android image, the device must be a **VMware Ready** Android device. Today, there are several devices available that are VMware Ready, especially in Japan and the USA. In Europe, Middle East, and Africa the device manufactures and carriers are yet to pick up the opportunity on a wide scale. Sony was the first to offer a carrier-independent, worldwide VMware Ready device with their Xperia Z1 and Ultra Z models. No matter whether your carrier supports Horizon Workspace or not, one of these worldwide VMware Ready devices will support running the virtual corporate-managed Android image. Hopefully, many more device manufactures will jump on the train and offer worldwide VMware Ready devices. For the latest list of VMware Ready devices, please refer to the following link: `http://www.vmware.com/files/pdf/VMware-ready-devices.pdf`.

VMware Horizon Workspace 1.5 has some other capabilities when it comes to mobile management as well. VMware offers native apps for both the Android and iOS platform available for download via Google Play or the Apple App Store. These apps are Horizon Workspace and Horizon Files (iOS only). The Horizon Workspace application allows a user to access their web-based applications as well as their VMware View Desktops. The Horizon Workspace app supports **Single Sign-On (SSO)** to web applications supporting **Security Assertion Markup Language (SAML)**. On Android, the Horizon Workspace app offers access to Horizon Files as well.

The Horizon Files application allows the users to access their Horizon Files documents on an iOS device. Horizon Workspace allows the synchronization of documents locally to the device. Locally-synced files are stored in an encrypted and secured separate area on the device. The Horizon Files module of Horizon Workspace is discussed in more detail in *Chapter 3, Horizon Files*. The Horizon Workspace and the Horizon Files app can be used on all later Android and iOS devices. There is no need for a VMware Ready device in order to use them. An IT administrator can specify policies such as device password and data containment and also perform a remote wipe of the locally synchronized files if a device is lost or stolen.

From the Horizon Workspace app, an IT administrator can recommend certain apps to their users. These are called **referred** apps. This is basically a link to an app in the Google Play Store or the Apple App Store. This makes it easier for the end users to download the correct app onto their device. The administrator cannot manage these referred apps.

Configuring Mobile Management

Let's start by taking a look at how to enable the Mobile Management component in Horizon Workspace 1.5.

First, we need to access the Horizon Workspace Admin portal. So, open a browser, go to the address `https://FQDN_to_Workspace/Admin`, and log in as the Horizon administrator. Enable the **Mobile Management** module by clicking on the green **Enable this module** button (1), as shown in the following screenshot:

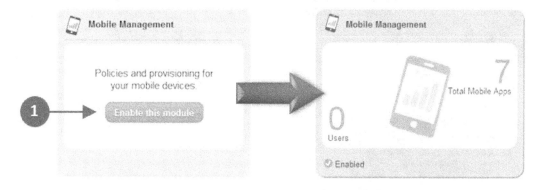

Once the module is activated, you can access the catalog to see the virtual Android images that are shipped by default with Horizon Workspace 1.5. This is shown in the following screenshot:

Click on the orange VMware Android Workspace image (1) to entitle users to it. In the following screenshot, you can see that we have entitled the user **Test User1** to the image:

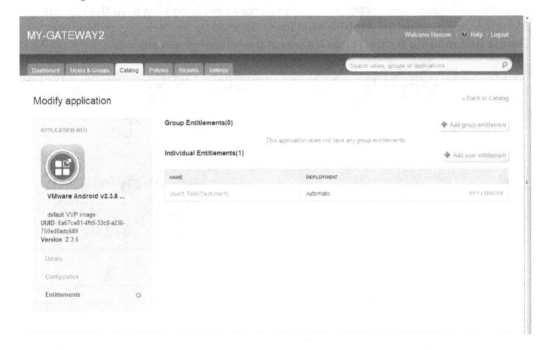

Next, click on one of the included Android apps to manage entitlement. This is shown in the following screenshot.

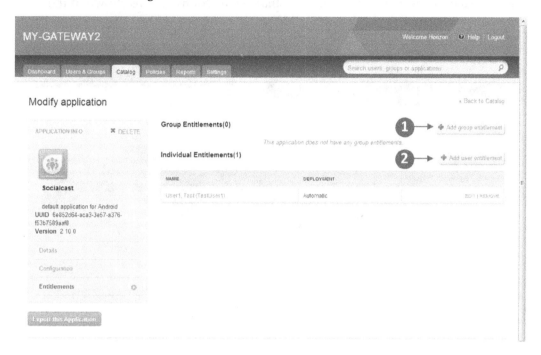

Horizon Workspace comes with some business apps that the administrator can deploy to the virtual Android image, for example, Socialcast. Once an application is entitled to a user (**2**), the application will be deployed to the corporate image. An IT administrator can add Android apps to Horizon Workspace by uploading the **Android application package** (**APK**) files. You could also entitle a group of users (**1**).

Later in this chapter, we'll have a look at mobile device enrollment; but first, let's have a look at some of the mobile policies available in Horizon Workspace.

Horizon Mobile Workspace policies

There are a number of mobile policy sets that can be configured as shown in the following screenshot:

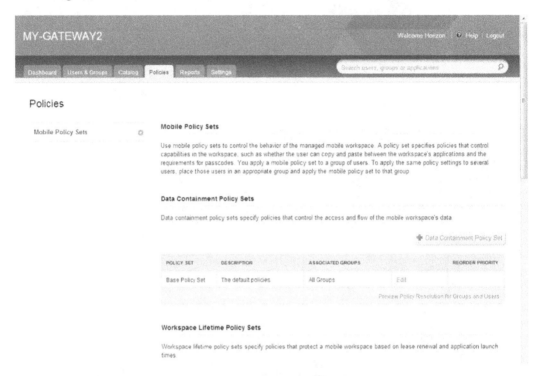

In the Horizon Workspace admin portal, click on the **Policies** tab to configure **Mobile Policy Sets**. The following policy sets are available:

- **Data Containment Policy Sets**: This policy dictates how corporate data can be protected, for example, whether copy and paste is allowed or not.

- **Workspace Lifetime Policy Sets**: This specifies for how long an authenticated session/Workspace will be allowed to be kept logged in before the user must authenticate again.

- **Passcode Policy Sets**: This dictates the complexity requirements of the password and timeout.

- **Secure Network Access Policy Sets**: This policy allows an admin to specify a VPN tunnel to always be activated for the virtual Android phone. This way all communications done by the corporate phone are passed through the VPN connection.

While working with multiple policies, it can soon become difficult to know which policies are applied to which users. To help solve this problem, each policy set has a **Preview Policy Resolution for Groups and Users** feature. So, you can see the result of what is applied to the user, as shown in the following screenshot:

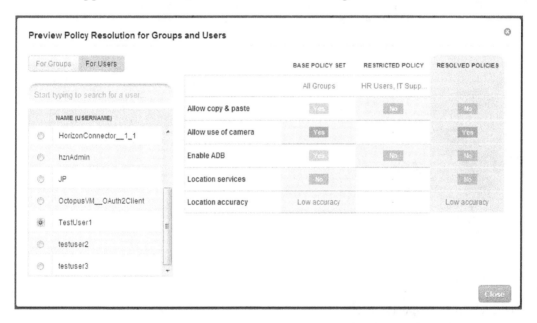

Each Horizon Files **Class of Service (COS)** has its own subset of mobile policies as well. For each Horizon Files COS, you can specify some mobile policies as shown in the following screenshot:

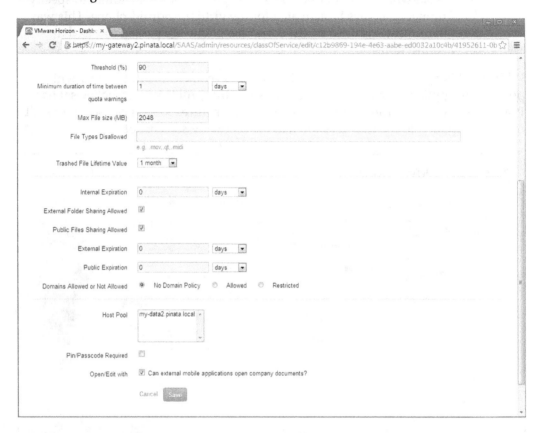

For each COS property, you can specify whether a PIN/passcode is required on the device and whether the Horizon Files app is allowed to share files with other apps on the phone. These mobile policies are for the Horizon Files mobile app. It does not rely on the end user device being a managed Android device. Both iOS Horizon Files and Android Horizon Workspace apps are affected by these COS policies.

Mobile device enrolment

After you have set up the policies and entitlements, it's time to enroll the user's mobiles.

Enrolling an Android device

Let us start with a VMware Ready Android device; a Sony Xperia Z1 in this case.

Start by launching the Google Play Store, locating the VMware Switch application, and then installing the app. If VMware Switch is not found, this means that your device is not a VMware Ready device.

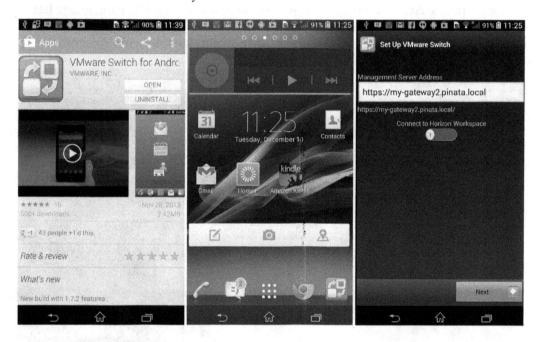

The previous screenshots show the App Store, the installed Switch app, and then how to configure your workspace.

Once the VMware Switch application is installed, launch it; the URL to your Horizon Workspace server is asked in the beginning. Specify the server URL and hit **Next**. To connect your device to the Horizon Workspace server successfully, your device must trust the certificate used. It is recommended that you use a certificate signed by a public Internet **Certificate Authority** (**CA**). If you use the default self-signed certificate, make sure that you first download and install the root certificate that can be found at the following URL: `https://FQDN_to_Workspace/horizon_workspace_rootca.pem`.

Next, sign in to your Mobile Workspace as a valid Horizon Workspace user who is entitled to a VMware Android image. Accept the license agreement and then wait for the corporate Android image to download onto the device. Once the image has been successfully downloaded onto your device, you will be notified. Then, you can launch VMware Switch again. This process is shown in the following screenshots:

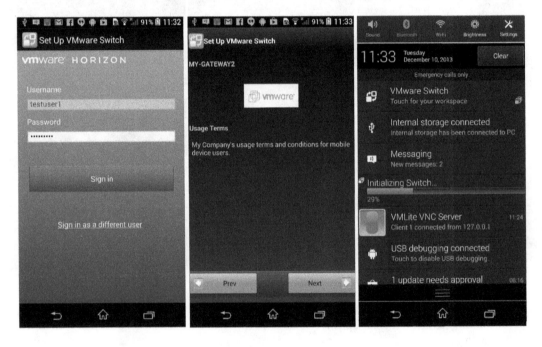

The first time you launch your corporate Android image, you will be prompted for a password. This is the password policy specified in Horizon Workspace. After entering your password, you will have access to your corporate-managed Android image, as shown in the following screenshots:

If you search the available apps on the Android image, you can see the applications entitled to your image by the Horizon admin. An end user cannot install any applications on the corporate image.

If your Android is not a VMware Ready device, you can still install the Horizon Workspace app on your phone. This app provides access to Horizon Files, web-based apps, and referred apps as shown in the following screenshot:

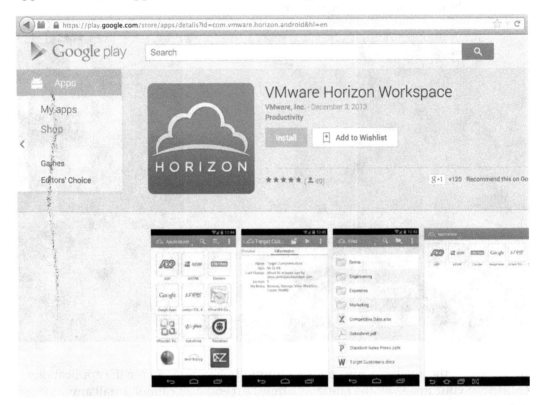

Enrolling an iOS device

Let's take a look at the Horizon apps for iOS. There are two Horizon apps available that support Horizon Workspace 1.5 on iOS: one for Horizon Workspace and another for Horizon Files. In the Horizon Workspace app, users can access their entitled web-based applications and find any iOS apps referred by the admin. Horizon Files allows the user to access their Horizon Files documents and access Horizon View desktops.

Start by downloading the two apps from the Apple App store.

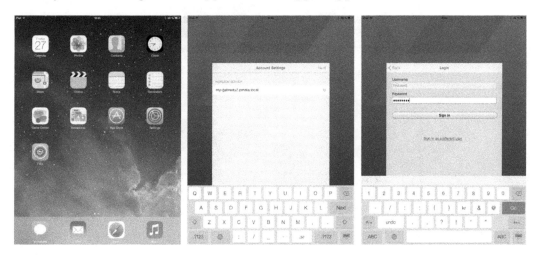

In the previous screenshots, you can see the installation of the Horizon apps. The setup is pretty much identical for the two applications, so let's have a closer look at Horizon Files.

When you launch Horizon Files for the first time, you are asked for the Horizon Workspace server URL. Make sure your iOS device trusts the certificate used by Horizon Workspace. It is recommended that you use a proper, publicly-signed certificate. If using the default self-signed certificate, make sure that you install it on your iOS device. You install the self-signed certificate by simply launching the Safari browser on your iOS device and navigating to `https://FQDN_to_Workspace/ horizon_workspace_rootca.pem`.

Accept to install the certificate and you should be good to go.

Log in to Horizon Workspace. You will see the following screenshot:

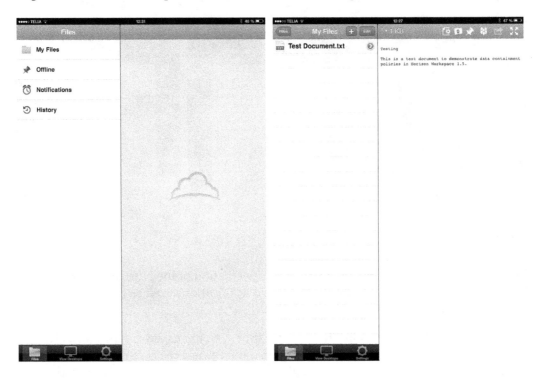

Once you are signed in, you will see your Horizon Files documents. In this example, we only have one file. Looking at the screenshot on the right-hand side, at its top-right corner you can see the Open-In icon being grayed out. This is because the policy is set to not allow Horizon Files to share externally. The only way the user can consume data is by using Horizon Files and the built-in preview functionality to view the data. In this way, a company can contain their data being accessed using mobile devices.

Click on the View Desktop tab and you will be presented with your enrolled VMware Horizon View desktop images. VMware Horizon View integration is discussed in more detail in *Chapter 7, Horizon View Integration*. If you do not have the native Horizon View client on your device, Safari will be used to access your desktop using the HTML5 remote protocol called Blast. If you have the View client installed on your device, you will be connected to your desktop using the native View client.

Summary

In this chapter, we described the Mobile Management functionalities in Horizon Workspace 1.5. We learned how to specify policies as well as how to deploy a corporate virtual Android image and how to install and configure Horizon Files on an iOS device.

In the next chapter, we will discuss how to integrate the ThinApp packages into Horizon Workspace.

6
Integrating ThinApp Packages

In this chapter, we'll look at how to manage Windows-based applications in Horizon Workspace 1.5. While web-based applications and mobile apps are quickly making their way into the corporate application estate, Windows-based applications will be around for many years to come. A popular method of packaging Windows applications for easier deployment, maintenance, and support is to virtualize them using application virtualization. Once virtualized, you don't have to install the application in order to use it. You simply execute the application. Many vendors offer application virtualization, but the two main players are Microsoft with App-V and VMware with ThinApp. Horizon Workspace supports VMware ThinApp-packaged Windows applications. If you are interested in learning more about application packaging using VMware ThinApp, *Packt Publishing* has this great book on the topic (the free chapter offers a quick overview of ThinApp), *VMware ThinApp 4.7 Essentials*, at http://www.packtpub.com/vmware-thinapp-4-7-essentials/book.

An overview of ThinApp integration

ThinApp support in Horizon Workspace relies on clients having the Horizon Agent installed locally. The Horizon Agent is used for both Horizon Files' local synchronization, and also for ThinApp deployment and entitlement. In this book, we are using Horizon Agent Version 1.5.2.

If you are using the Horizon Agent only for ThinApp entitlements, you can disable the Horizon Files synchronization feature using the following command during the installation of the agent:

```
VMware-Horizon -Workspace-1.x.x-XXXX.exe /v ENABLE_DATA=0
```

There are two different deployment methods supported in Horizon Workspace 1.5: local deployment method and streaming deployment method. Local deployment means that the ThinApp packages are copied down to the client's hard disk and executed from there. Streaming is when users stream the packaged Windows application from a network share. Streaming is still executing on the local client, but all the bits necessary to execute the application are downloaded when requested.

Streaming is typically used in a **Virtual Desktop Infrastructure (VDI)** implementation. Streaming the packages allows users to use the application without the need to install it on each VDI desktop. Local deployment is most suitable in a physical client environment. The ThinApp packages are deployed locally to the device's hard disk and can, therefore, be used offline.

It is the agent settings that decide which deployment method the client will use. While you can change the settings after the fact, via the registry, it is normally during installation that you specify the deployment method.

The local deployment installation parameter is as follows:

```
VMware-Horizon -Workspace-1.x.x-XXXX.exe /s /v HORIZONURL=https://
Gateway_FQDN DOWNLOAD=1 POLLINGINTERVAL=3600
```

The streaming deployment installation parameter is as follows:

```
VMware-Horizon -Workspace-1.x.x-XXXX.exe /s /v HORIZONURL=https://
Gateway_FQDN DOWNLOAD=0 POLLINGINTERVAL=3600
```

The DOWNLOAD parameter decides whether packages are to be downloaded locally to the client or not. In the preceding examples, we are specifying a polling interval of 3600 seconds. This specifies how often the agent will contact the Horizon Workspace server to poll for new entitlements. If users are entitled to an application not using the automatic entitlement option, they can entitle themselves to a ThinApp package using the web portal. Users can immediately launch the ThinApp package even though the Horizon Agent has not yet synchronized the new entitlement. If a ThinApp package is launched from the web portal and no active entitlement exists, then the Horizon Agent will force a synchronization to check for new entitlements.

The Horizon Agent keeps a local database of all user entitlements. The default location is in the user's local profile, %LOCALAPPDATA%\ VMware\Horizon ThinApp\InstallDb.ini.

If you have deployed the Horizon Agent using the local deployment method, it is in the PackageCache folder under %LOCALAPPDATA%\ VMware\Horizon ThinApp, where your local copies of the ThinApp packages will be located. All paths can be changed from the default settings.

Enabling Horizon management in your ThinApp packages

In order for your ThinApp packages to be able to be managed by Horizon Workspace, you must activate Horizon Workspace management within your packages. The following are the three methods to achieve this:

- During the capturing of your Windows application.

  In Setup Capture, you can specify the package to be managed using Horizon Workspace.

- Manually add the following Horizon Workspace parameters in your package's `package.ini` file and rebuild your project folder:

  ```
  ;-------- Horizon Parameters ----------
  AppID=genid
  NotificationDLLs=HorizonPlugin.dll
  ```

- Run `relink.exe` using the `-h` parameter.

  You can activate the Horizon Workspace management on the existing packages without the need to rebuild the whole project folder. Simply execute `relink.exe -h PathToPackage\Package.exe` and relink will inject Horizon management into the package.

 If you use relink and your package contains multiple entry points and a separate data container, it is important to run `relink.exe -h` using `PathToPackage\*.*`. This way, all entry points and the data container get the same AppID.

Once Horizon Workspace management has been activated on a ThinApp package, you cannot execute the package without the Horizon Agent or without an active entitlement from Horizon Workspace.

Enabling ThinApp integration in Horizon Workspace

The first thing to do is activate the ThinApp module. To enable the ThinApp module, click on the green **Enable this module** button (1). This is shown in the following screenshot:

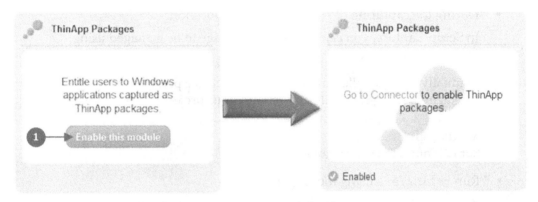

Once the module has been activated, you must configure the ThinApp repository. The connector-va appliance is responsible for the ThinApp repository synchronization. The connector-va appliance will poll the file share where you have placed your ThinApp packages and synchronize the metadata into the service catalog. Once the packages are present in the catalog, the administrator can entitle users to them. The connector-va appliance only supports accessing a standard Windows file server share. Since the connector uses its Active Directory computer account to access the file share, appropriate permissions must exist. Whether the ThinApp packages are deployed locally or using streaming, it is the end user, through the Horizon Agent, accessing the packages on the network share. So, not only does the connector-va appliance need to have the correct permissions, the users should have them as well. An easy approach is to simply give authenticated users read and execute permissions to the share. This will deal with both the connector-va's access as well as your end users' access.

When you populate your ThinApp share, it is important that all ThinApp packages live within their own subfolders. For example, if your ThinApp repository share is called \\ServerName\ThinAppShare, then a valid path for the deployment of the package is \\ServerName\ThinAppShare\Mozilla Firefox\Firefox.exe.

It is not recommended that you place packages in the root directory of the share nor can you have more than one folder deep. You should upload only your package files, entry points and data containers (.exe and .dat files). Horizon Workspace does not use MSI-wrapped packages.

In Horizon Workspace 1.5, the ThinApp repository cannot be a Microsoft **Distributed File System (DFS)** share; it must be a standard Windows file share.

ThinApp configuration in Horizon Workspace

Earlier, we discussed some of the prerequisites for delivering ThinApp packages from Horizon Workspace. In this section, we will configure them.

Log in to the connector-va appliance using the Horizon admin account. The URL for connector-va is `https://FQDN_to_Connector:8443`, as shown in the following screenshot:

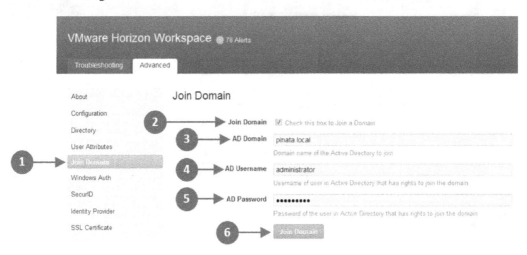

You must join your connector-va appliance to your domain so that it can access the network share. On your connector-va appliance, click on **Join Domain** (**1**) from the left-hand side menu options. Next, check the **Join Domain** checkbox (**2**) and then fill in the following details:

- Enter your domain name. In our example, the domain is `pinata.local`.
- Enter **AD Username**. Specify an account with privileges to join computers to the domain. You can create the computer account ahead of time if you are in a highly secure environment. The computer account name will be the hostname of your connector-va appliance.
- Enter the password for this account.

Once you have filled in the details, click on the green **Join Domain** button (**6**).

[The username and password used to join the connector-va appliance to the domain will not be stored. They are only used to join the domain.]

Next, we will configure the location of the ThinApp packages.

From the left-hand side menu, click on **ThinApp Packages** (**1**), as shown in the following screenshot:

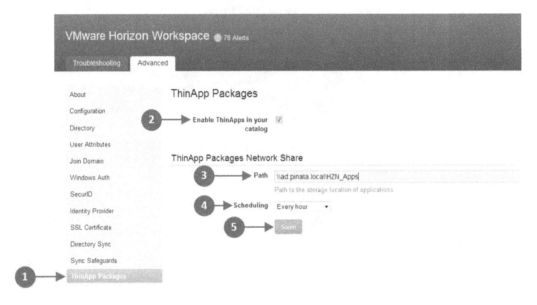

Tick **Enable ThinApps in your catalog** (**2**).

Then, type **Path** (**3**) to the network share where your ThinApp packages live and then choose a **Scheduling** period (**4**). This is how often Horizon Workspace will look for new ThinApp packages and entitlements. Finally, click on the green **Save** button (**5**).

The connector-va appliance will now scan the ThinApp repository and synchronize all packages' metadata to the Horizon Workspace catalog so that you can entitle end users to the packages.

To check the catalog and the ThinApps that have been synchronized, log in to the Workspace as the administrator using `https://my-gateway2.pinata.local/Admin`.

Click on the **Catalog** tab (**1**) and then click on **ThinApp Packages** (**2**) from the left-hand side menu, as shown in the following screenshot. This is where we can now start to entitle end users to the packages.

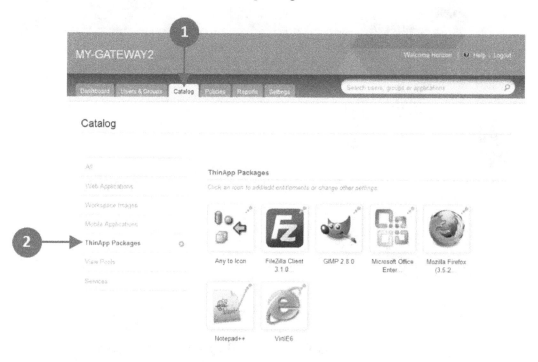

Entitling a user to the ThinApp-packaged application

Once your ThinApp packages are synchronized, they are shown in the **Catalog** tab. In order to entitle a user to an application, first click on the application's icon. In the following example, we have selected Microsoft Office, as shown in the following screenshot:

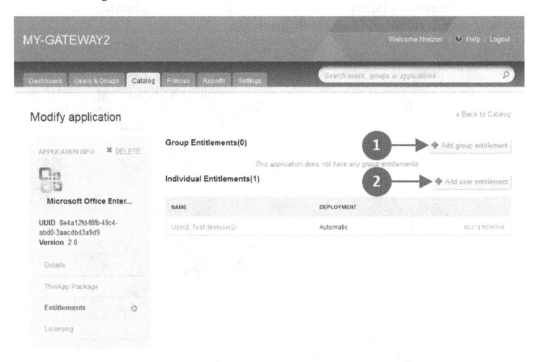

We can either add groups or users. Click on **+ Add group entitlements** to add a group to this application or click on **+ Add user entitlement** to add an individual user. In our example, we have entitled the **TestUser2** account and set the deployment type to **Automatic**. This means that the Microsoft Office ThinApp package will appear in the user's main Workspace page by default.

Updating ThinApp packages

Horizon Workspace supports distributing updates to ThinApp packages. Horizon Workspace uses the package.ini parameters, AppID= and VersionID=, to identify a new version of a package. When deploying the new version of a package, you should place it in a new folder on the ThinApp share. The connector-va appliance will pick it up during synchronization, and the new version will be automatically distributed to the end users.

The following screenshot shows an example of two package.ini files: one is the original version, VersionID=1, and the second is the updated package, VersionID=2. You must use an integer as the VersionID value.

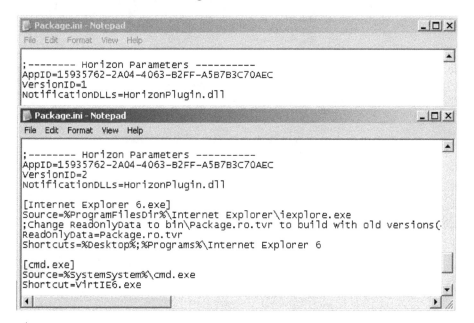

Another method to create an updated ThinApp package is to use relink.exe. You can run relink.exe -h -VersionID + to increment VersionID automatically. For a full list of supported relink.exe parameters, simply run relink.exe without any parameters.

Summary

In this chapter, we discussed how to activate and configure ThinApp integration in Horizon Workspace. We also covered how to activate Horizon Workspace management in ThinApp packages and the different deployment methods supported in Horizon Workspace 1.5.

In the following chapter, we will look at how to integrate VMware Horizon View in Horizon Workspace.

7
Horizon View Integration

So far in this book, we have discussed how Horizon Workspace delivers a single web-based user interface that allows users to access files, **Software as a Service (SaaS)** applications, ThinApp packages, and mobile applications. In this chapter, we will cover the last component that a user can access, and that's their virtual desktop.

Configuring Horizon Workspace for view access

The first thing that we need to do is enable the Horizon View module and then configure the View elements from within Horizon Workspace. You will also need a VMware Horizon View 5.2 or newer deployment already up and running.

We will need to perform the following steps to set up the basic configurations:

1. Log on to the configurator-va appliance as the Horizon Administrator.
2. From the options on the left-hand side, select **Module Configuration**.
3. Click on the **Enable this module** button (**1**). This is shown in the following screenshot:

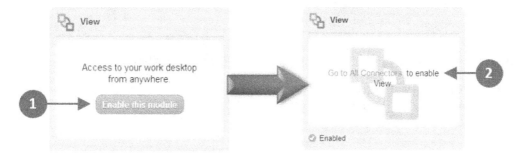

4. Once enabled, you will see that there is a link to the connector-va appliance (**2**). Clicking on this link will take you directly to the connector appliance, which we need to do in order to complete the next steps in the configuration process and configure the user access and Horizon View pools.

5. Click on **Go to All Connectors** (**2**). You will see the screenshot shown in the next section. On this screen, the first task we will complete is configuring the user accounts.

Configuring user accounts for Horizon View

Horizon View requires the **userPrincipalName** (UPN) attribute to be enabled for users to log on to their desktops. So, we need to add this to the **Map User Attributes** configuration page for Horizon Workspace. We covered this in *Chapter 2, Design, Install, and Configure,* but as a quick reminder, you will find the following screenshot:

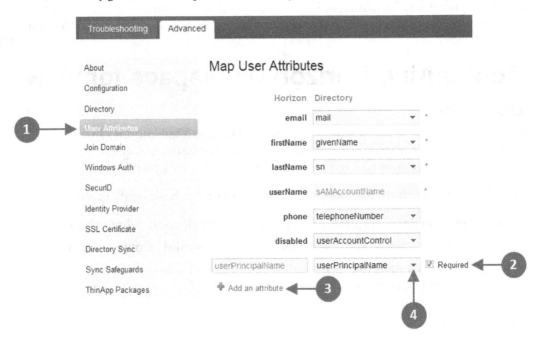

We need to perform the following steps to configure the attributes:

1. Click on **User Attributes** (**1**), and then make sure that you check the box next to the option for **userPrincipalName** (**2**).

2. If this attribute is not already configured, then you will need to add it to the list. To do this, click on **Add an attribute** (**3**), and then from the drop-down box (**4**), select the appropriate attribute. In this case, it's **userPrincipalName**.

3. Click on the green **Save** button when you have completed the configuration.

Enabling and configuring Horizon View pools

The next step is to configure Horizon Workspace to read the information from the Horizon View Connection Servers, namely the pool information, as that is what gets presented in the user's Workspace. A desktop pool is a collection of desktops that are configured identically. This approach allows IT admins to centralize desktop management and simplify the configuration. It also allows you to deploy identical applications to specific groups of users and to automate virtual desktop provisioning.

This is also completed from the connector-va appliance, as shown in the following screenshot:

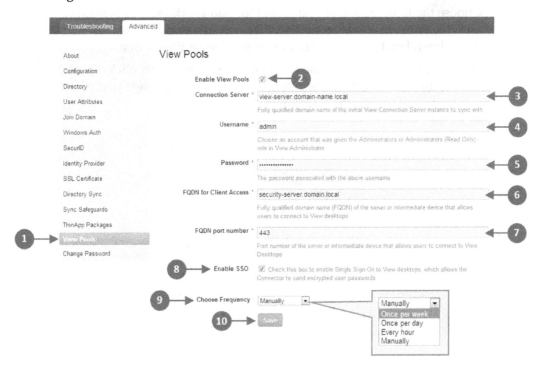

Enter the configuration details as follows:

1. Click on **View Pools** from the left-hand side menu options, as shown in the preceding screenshot.

2. Then, check the **Enable View Pools** box to show the configuration page.

3. Enter the **Fully Qualified Domain Name (FQDN)** of your Horizon View Connection Server.

4. Enter the username of an account with read-only access to View.

5. Enter the password of the account that we configured earlier.

6. If you have a View Security Server, then enter the address here. If not, then use the View Connection Server address.

7. Enter the port number required for users to connect to the preceding address.

8. To enable Single Sign-On to the View desktop, check the box to the right-hand side of **Enable SSO**.

9. Choose the frequency that you want Horizon Workspace to synchronize with the Horizon View Connection Servers. The options are shown in the drop-down box to the right-hand side of **Choose Frequency**.

10. Once you have completed the configuration information, click on the green **Save** button. You will see the information in the following screenshot:

View Pools

	REPLICATED SERVER GROUP	PORT NUMBER	SSL CERT	SAML AUTH INFO	ADMIN CONSOLE
	view.	443	Update SSL Cert	SAML Auth enabled	Admin Console

This information confirms that Horizon Workspace can communicate with Horizon View. From here, you can also automatically launch the View Administrator by clicking on the link. You do not need to sign in again.

Once the information has been confirmed, the last step is to synchronize the Horizon View desktop pool information to Horizon Workspace, as shown in the following screenshot. Click on the **Sync Now >>** button (**1**).

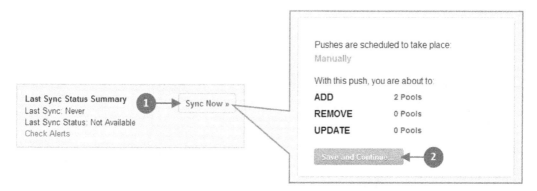

Check the tasks to be performed, especially if pools are going to be removed. Click on **Save and Continue...** (**2**) to perform the synchronization. You will see a message as shown in the following screenshot:

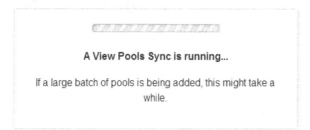

If you now return to the gateway-va appliance, log in as the Horizon Administrator, and look at the dashboard; you will see that we have Horizon View desktop pools and users entitled to use them, as shown in the following screenshot:

We have now completed the Horizon Workspace part of the configuration. The next step, covered in the next section, is to make some configuration changes in the View Administrator.

Configuring the Horizon View Workspace integration

To connect to a Horizon View desktop from your Horizon Workspace web page, Horizon Workspace uses **Security Assertion Markup Language (SAML)** as its authentication mechanism. We discussed the use of SAML-based authentication in *Chapter 4, Integrating SaaS Applications*.

In this section, we are going to configure the desktop access.

Configuring SAML authentication

Launch the Horizon View Administrator console and log in with an account that has the permission to edit the View configuration settings. As previously discussed, you can launch the Horizon View Administrator by clicking on the link on the **View Pools** page on the connector-va appliance.

The first thing we need to do is add Horizon Workspace as a method of authentication for Horizon View by following the steps described and shown in the next screenshot.

From the View Administrator screen, click on **Servers** (1), and then click on the tab for **Connection Servers** (2). Highlight the relevant Connection Server (3), and then click on the **Edit...** button (4).

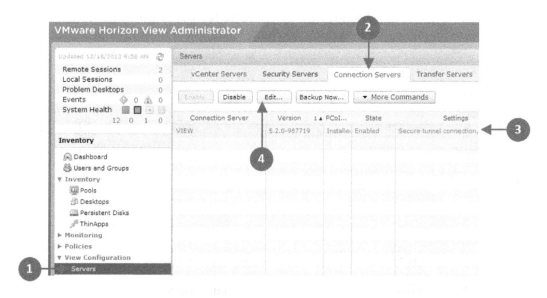

In the **Edit View Connection Server Settings** dialog box shown in the following screenshot, click on the **Authentication** tab (1).

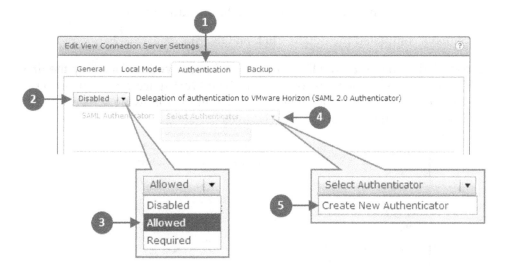

First we need to enable the delegation of authentication. To do this, click on the drop-down menu (**2**) and select the option **Allowed** (**3**). Next, we need to create the authenticator.

Click on the drop-down menu (**4**) and select **Create New Authenticator** (**5**). You will see the following dialog box in which you have to complete the authenticator details:

Complete the details to add a SAML authenticator as follows:

- **Label** (**1**): This is the display name for this authenticator
- **Description** (**2**): Type in a more detailed description
- **Metadata URL** (**3**): Insert the URL for Horizon Workspace
- **Administration URL** (**4**): Optionally add the admin URL

Once you have completed the details, click on **OK** (**5**).

When completing the **Metadata URL** details, make sure you replace only the first part of the address with the name of your Horizon Workspace server, ensuring that you leave the rest of the URL intact as shown in the following screenshot. Just change the address in between the two red lines.

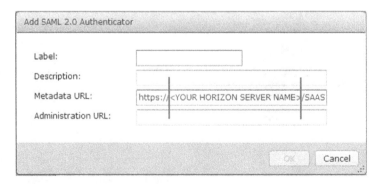

You should now have a working solution and be able to access the Horizon View desktops that you are entitled to. In the next section, we will demonstrate this.

Configuring HTML5 desktop access

One of the methods for accessing your desktop from Horizon Workspace is by using an HTML5 compatible browser. This feature was introduced in Horizon View 5.2. From their Horizon Workspace, you can now allow a user to access their desktop either from a compatible browser or View Client.

In order to provide browser access, you first need to install the Horizon View Feature Pack directly onto the Horizon View Connection Server. This enables the VMware Blast protocol.

To do this, you need to go to the **VMware Horizon View Administrator** console, and then navigate to **View Configuration | Servers | Connection Servers**. Right-click on the appropriate Connection Server.

Then, navigate to **Pools**, select the pool you want to allow HTML5 web access to, and click on **Edit...**. Finally, select the **Pool Settings** tab, and check the box to the right-hand side of **HTML Access (1)** as shown in the following screenshot:

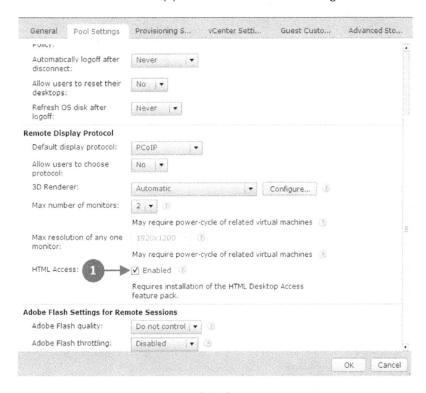

For more information on the Horizon View Feature Pack, visit the following link: `http://tinyurl.com/oye378r`.

Accessing your desktop

We should now be able to access Horizon View desktops from Horizon Workspace.

Before we test this, it's worth just checking whether the users in Horizon Workspace have been entitled to desktops and are also entitled in Horizon View Administrator.

Log in to Horizon Workspace with a user that is entitled to a desktop pool in Horizon View. In this example, we will use the Test User2 account.

Click on the **View Desktops** tab (**1**) as shown in the following screenshot. Now right-click on the graphic and you will see there are two options. The first one (**2**) opens your desktop with Horizon View Client. If you don't have it installed, it will display a **download** button, which will take you to the download page on the VMware website. The second option (**3**) is to open your Horizon View desktop in a browser.

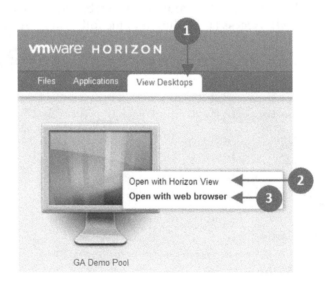

Summary

In this chapter, we discussed how to configure access to your Horizon View desktops directly from your Horizon Workspace.

You should now be able to enable the Horizon View module, configure the desktop pools, and also add an authenticator to Horizon View to allow Horizon Workspace to connect to your virtual desktop.

We have now covered all the components of Horizon Workspace and demonstrated how everything can be accessed from just a single URL, whether it be SaaS apps from a cloud provider, ThinApp packages, files and data, mobile devices (both iOS and Android), or a complete virtual desktop.

In the next chapter, we will discuss some of the most common troubleshooting tips.

8
Troubleshooting

In this chapter, we'll have a look at the common issues and possible solutions when installing and deploying Horizon Workspace from appliances to clients. We will also look at how to access the logs of different appliances.

Installation troubleshooting

First, let's have a look at some of the common issues during the initial setup of Horizon Workspace.

Networking

The most common errors that prevent successful installation are around getting the networking elements to work. We'll cover the two most common problems that we encounter.

Configuring the IP pool

First, verify your IP pool. The IP pool requirements have been discussed in *Chapter 2, Design, Install, and Configure*, but since it is a common problem, it is worth mentioning one more time. The Horizon Workspace vApp picks up your network properties such as default gateway, DNS server, and domain name from the IP-Pool.

Verify that your IP pool looks something like the following screenshot:

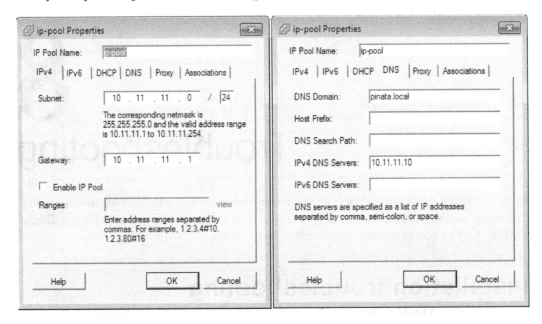

The only things that you should have defined in your IP pool are the **Subnet**, **Gateway**, **DNS Domain**, and one DNS server. An IP pool supports multiple DNS servers, but the Horizon Workspace installer does not. Finally, make sure you have the association made to the network that you plan to connect your vApp to.

 Remember, all the virtual appliances in the vApp must be connected to the same network segment. It is not supported to have them on different networks.

DNS errors

It's very common to experience DNS issues right at the beginning of the **Command-Line Interface (CLI)** setup, before you even get started with the setup wizard part of the installation.

The example in the following screenshot shows a typical error during the setup of the configurator-va appliance, where it begins to resolve the IP addressed to get the hostnames:

```
     - vCenter Server admin user (such as root for Linux, Administrator for Windo
ws).
     - Password for the vCenter Server admin user.
     - SMTP server to use for sending messages.


          Proceed? Press Enter to continue:
Verifying network environment
Discovering network configuration:
  DNS server=10.11.11.10, gateway=10.11.11.1, netmask=255.255.255.0

Check configurator-va 10.11.11.55
  DNS found = my-configurator2.pinata.local
Check connector-va 10.11.11.57
  DNS found = my-connector2.pinata.local
Check data-va 10.11.11.58
  DNS found = my-data2.pinata.local
Check gateway-va 10.11.11.59
  DNS found = my-gateway2.pinata.local
Check service-va 10.11.11.56
Failed to lookup IP list for 10.11.11.56
    Reverse DNS failure and/or DNS mismatch for 10.11.11.56
Errors detected, you must correct them before installation can proceed.
The system must be restarted after the errors are corrected.
Press enter to shut down the VM_
```

As you can see, there is an issue with the reverse lookup for the IP address 10.11.11.56, which is for the service-va appliance. In this case, we have simply added two PTR records (pointer records) to the reverse lookup zone, both pointing to different hostnames. There should only be one PTR per IP address. In this case, to solve the issue, we need to check the DNS settings. Another common issue is that there are no reverse lookup zones at all.

> To verify the reverse lookup without restarting the appliance, you could run the nslookup command from a Windows command line. For example, in the previous error, we could use nslookup 10.11.11.56.
>
> Also make sure that you read the error message carefully when you get one. Often, the error messages are quite good and informative, and can point you in the right direction when it comes to troubleshooting.

Web-based setup wizard issues

The most common mistake when it comes to the web-based part of the setup is the lack of understanding of the integration to the **Active Directory (AD)**.

Troubleshooting AD errors

One of the most common issues when configuring the AD components in Horizon Workspace is missing user attributes in the user account, such as not having an e-mail address entered. The following screenshot shows the **Directory** configuration page and a typical error message relating to a missing attribute. In this case, it's a missing e-mail address.

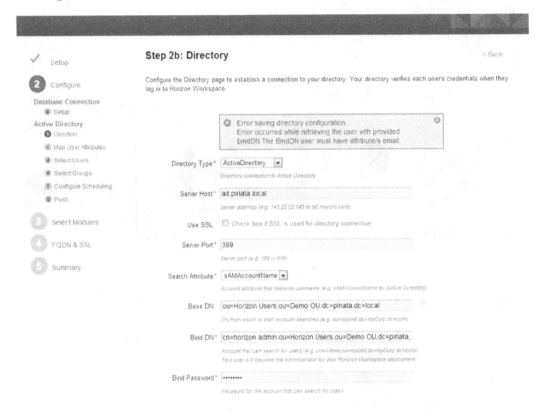

In the example in the previous screenshot, the **Bind DN** user does not have the email attribute specified. Horizon Workspace depends heavily on the user's email attribute, and therefore the email attribute is also required for the **Bind DN** user.

Another issue can be the search path that you have entered. If we take the previous example, we are using the following as the **Bind DN** user:

```
cn=hzn admin,ou=Horizon Users,ou=Demo OU,dc=pinata,dc=local
```

Basically, this translated Bind DN is looking for the `hzn admin` user account located in the `Horizon Users` OU, which in turn is in the `Demo OU` container in the domain `pinata.local`. This example uses a separate OU (user) for our Horizon users.

If you are planning on using a user account, that is, in the `Users` part of your AD, then it's important to know that the users are not an OU but a CN. For example, if you want to specify that the Administrator account be the Bind DN user, you must specify the following search path:

```
cn=Administrator,cn=Users,dc=pinata,dc=local
```

User-synchronization issues

You must make sure that when you import users to Horizon Workspace, the filter does not delete your Bind DN user. The following screenshot depicts the pushes that are scheduled to take place:

In the previous screenshot, you can see that one user is listed as being removed (**1**). This indicates that you are about to delete your Bind DN user from Horizon Workspace. Since the Base DN user is the first administrator in Horizon Workspace, this is not something you would want to do, as you would not be able to log in and administer the Workspace. Make sure that the initial directory synchronization never has any users listed as being removed. If your filter is set up correctly, you will have a couple of additions and one user listed as being updated.

Time-synchronization issues

Horizon Workspace internally uses **Security Assertion Markup Language (SAML)** for authentication between the different appliances. Since SAML is very time sensitive in its nature, with its assertions having a **Time To Live (TTL)** of 60 seconds, there can only be a maximum time drift of 30 seconds between the different appliances. One example of a time synchronization issue is that the end users cannot sign in. The following screenshot shows the error message received when login fails:

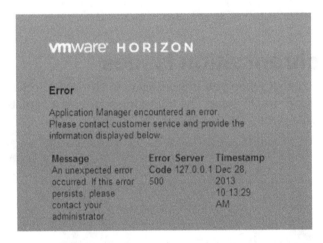

The error message that you receive when login fails, as shown in the previous screenshot, is not very informative. In order to identify a time synchronization issue, log in to the configurator-va appliance and click on **System Information**. You will see the following screenshot:

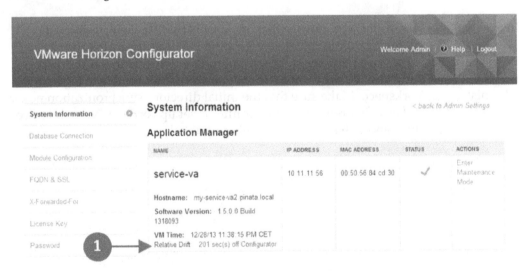

The previous login issue was due to the service-va appliance not being time synchronized with the rest of the vApp appliances. This is shown very clearly on the configurator-va **System Information** screen (**1**). Correct time synchronization being set up on the ESX hosts helps sort out vApp time synchronization issues. All the appliances pick up their time from the ESX host with the following exception: if you have joined the connector-va appliance to your domain, it will start to synchronize its time with the AD server.

Therefore, it is good practice to set up your ESX hosts to synchronize time with your AD servers and set up your AD servers to use an external time server. If you don't have **Network Time Protocol (NTP)** already set up in your network have a look at this link: `http://www.pool.ntp.org/en/` for publicly available NTP servers.

Changing the Fully Qualified Domain Name

When you change the Horizon Workspace **Fully Qualified Domain Name (FQDN)**, you may receive many different error messages as shown in the following screenshot:

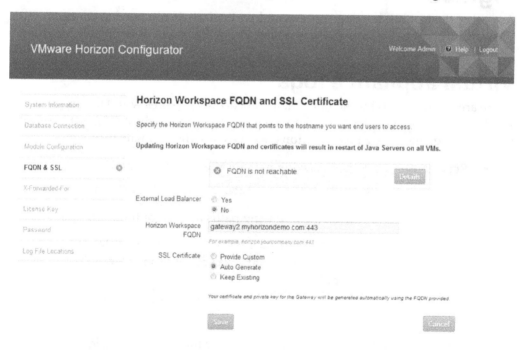

Pretty much all the issues that you may get during the change of the FQDN are related to communication issues. When changing the FQDN, all the appliances must be able to successfully communicate with the gateway-va appliance using the new FQDN and SSL. If the certificate is not trusted, you will not succeed in changing the FQDN.

A good practice when troubleshooting changing FQDN issues is to first verify the access using the FQDN in a web browser. Secondly, try to browse from each virtual appliance to the FQDN using cURL, a command-line-based browser: `http://curl.haxx.se/`.

Please remember, the only supported deployment method for external access to your Horizon Workspace is to use an external load balancer / reverse proxy between your external clients and the Horizon Workspace gateway. You should terminate the SSL certificate on the external load balancer. Therefore, it does not matter, if you keep the self-signed certificates on the Horizon Workspace appliances.

Accessing the Horizon Workspace logfiles

As part of the troubleshooting process, and particularly if you need to contact VMware support to help resolve any issues, you will need to download the logfiles.

Virtual appliance logs

There are many logs to investigate when you encounter issues with Horizon Workspace. All relevant logs and their locations are listed in the configurator-va web interface, under **Log File Locations**; we have also listed them as follows:

- **Service-va**: Check the following path for the service-va logfiles:
    - `/opt/vmware/horizon/horizoninstance/logs/horizon.log`

- **Configurator-va**: Check the following paths for the configurator-va logfiles:
    - `/opt/vmware/var/log/configurator-console.log`
    - `/opt/vmware/horizon/configuratorinstance/logs/configurator.log`
    - `/opt/vmware/horizon/configuratorinstance/logs/catalina.out`

- **Connector-va**: Check the following path for the connector-va logfiles:
    - `/opt/vmware/c2/c2instance/logs/connector.log`

- **Data-va (Horizon Files)**: Check the following paths for the data-va logfiles:
    - `/opt/zimbra/log/mailbox.log`
    - `/opt/zimbra/log/audit.log`
    - `/opt/zimbra/log/access.log`

Downloading the appliance logfiles

In order to read the logfiles, the easiest method is to open a **Secure Shell (SSH)** session into each virtual appliance using `SSHUSER` as the username. Then you will need to change user with the `su` (substitute user) command, changing to the `root` user. The command would look something like this:

```
su root
```

If you need to download logs from an appliance, you can use WinSCP. Since `root`, by default, does not have SSH access, make sure you first activate SSH access for the `root` user in `/etc/ssh/sshd_config` and issue the command `/etc/init.d/sshd restart`.

Client logfiles

Horizon Agents on all platforms allow you to collect logs for troubleshooting.

On the Mac Agent, you can collect the logs by clicking on the Horizon Agent icon on the menu bar and choosing **Preferences**. Here, you can click on the **Collect diagnostic information** button (**1**). The logs are collected and saved into a ZIP file, at the folder location (**2**), as shown in the following screenshot:

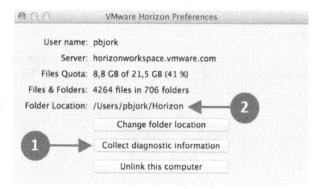

On Windows, you collect the logs in a similar fashion. Click on the Horizon Agent icon on the taskbar and choose **Options**. Then click on the **Collect diagnostic information** button (1). The logs are collected and saved into a ZIP file under the folder location, which by default is C:\Users\vmware\Horizon; however, you can change this location by clicking on **Change (2)**, as shown in the following screenshot:

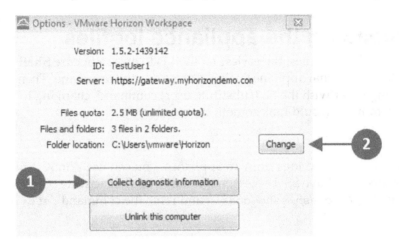

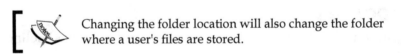

> Changing the folder location will also change the folder where a user's files are stored.

In the iOS Horizon Files app, you can collect logs from within the Settings menu and the option for **Upload logs to My Files**. The logs will be uploaded to the user's Horizon Files area.

Summary

In this chapter, we have walked you through some of the most common issues that IT administrators may come across when setting up and managing Horizon Workspace.

From experience, a majority of the issues are usually based on networking problems, particularly around DNS and AD, and how you have those elements deployed in your current infrastructure. Running a POC or pilot environment will help determine any changes you might need to make.

Useful Links

In this appendix, we will provide you with some additional information and useful links to find more information about VMware Horizon Workspace 1.5.

Community and blog pages

The community and blog pages can be found following these links:

- **Horizon Workspace community**: `http://tinyurl.com/o7r9mcf`
- **Horizon Workspace community documentation**: `http://tinyurl.com/psaztnf`

VMware official documentation

The main documentation page can be found via the following link:

`https://www.vmware.com/support/pubs/horizon-workspace-pubs.html`

The individual documents can be found using the following links:

- **Horizon Files command-line guide**: `http://tinyurl.com/omxoehf`
- **Installing and configuring Horizon Workspace**: `http://tinyurl.com/nup4d8d`
- **Upgrading Horizon Workspace**: `http://tinyurl.com/qglzq8y`
- **Horizon Workspace Administrator's Guide**: `http://tinyurl.com/o23n6rv`
- **Protection and Disaster recovery best practices for Horizon Files**: `http://tinyurl.com/ogeohg5`
- **Horizon Workspace user help**: `http://tinyurl.com/nkwoa7w`
- **Horizon Workspace user guide**: `http://tinyurl.com/nvajgc5`

- **Tips for fixing Workspace Client sync errors**:
  `http://tinyurl.com/proo12p`

- **Customizing Horizon Workspace**: `http://tinyurl.com/oc98amv`

- **Release notes**: `http://tinyurl.com/pd52rcx`

For more details on ThinApp and Horizon Workspace integration, please visit the official VMware ThinApp blog:

- `http://blogs.vmware.com/thinapp/horizon-workspace`

- `http://blogs.vmware.com/thinapp/integration/horizon`

Summary

In this appendix, we have listed just a few of the links to useful online resources that will help you configure, deploy, and manage your Horizon Workspace infrastructure and end users.

Index

H

Horizon Files
about 45
comments 63
document preview 57
files and folders, managing 59
history 68
synchronizing, with offline access 68-70
user accounts 56
version control 62, 63
Horizon Files module
enabling 48
users, entitling 49-51
Horizon Files storage resources
NFS data store, adding 48
storage, configuring on data-va virtual
machine 47
VMDK, adding to data-va appliance 47
Horizon management
enabling, in ThinApp packages 105
Horizon Mobile Workspace policies
configuring 92, 94
Horizon View
enabling 113
user accounts, configuring 114
view pools, configuring 115-117
view pools, enabling 115
Horizon View desktops
accessing 122
Horizon View Feature Pack
URL 122
Horizon View Workspace integration
configuring 118
SAML authentication, configuring 118-121
Horizon Workspace
about 7, 45
architecture 20
configuring, for SaaS apps 74
data appliance architecture 46
deployment 10
downloading 16
features 9
files 45
mobile management 87
multi-device access 70
prerequisites 11

sizing guide 20
technology, proving 11
ThinApp configuration 107
ThinApp integration 103
ThinApp integration, enabling 106
vApp 14
View elements, configuring 113, 114
virtual appliances (va) 15
web-based configuration 35
Horizon Workspace 1.5
community 135
community documentation 135
functionalities 9
Horizon Workspace Champions 16
Horizon Workspace logfiles
accessing 132
appliance logfiles, downloading 133
client logfiles 133, 134
virtual appliance logs 132
HTML5 desktop access
configuring 121, 122

I

**infrastructure requisites, for initial test set
up 11**
**infrastructure requisites, for production
deployment 12**
installation, troubleshooting
AD errors, troubleshooting 128
DNS Errors 126, 127
IP pool, configuring 125, 126
networking 125
time synchronization issues 130
user synchronization issues 129
web-based setup wizard issues 127
iOS app 72
iOS device
enrolling 98-100
IP pool, vApp
configuring 23-26

L

LibreOffice
about 57
installing 57

Thank you for buying
VMware Horizon Workspace Essentials

About Packt Publishing

Packt, pronounced 'packed', published its first book "Mastering phpMyAdmin for Effective MySQL Management" in April 2004 and subsequently continued to specialize in publishing highly focused books on specific technologies and solutions.

Our books and publications share the experiences of your fellow IT professionals in adapting and customizing today's systems, applications, and frameworks. Our solution based books give you the knowledge and power to customize the software and technologies you're using to get the job done. Packt books are more specific and less general than the IT books you have seen in the past. Our unique business model allows us to bring you more focused information, giving you more of what you need to know, and less of what you don't.

Packt is a modern, yet unique publishing company, which focuses on producing quality, cutting-edge books for communities of developers, administrators, and newbies alike. For more information, please visit our website: www.packtpub.com.

About Packt Enterprise

In 2010, Packt launched two new brands, Packt Enterprise and Packt Open Source, in order to continue its focus on specialization. This book is part of the Packt Enterprise brand, home to books published on enterprise software – software created by major vendors, including (but not limited to) IBM, Microsoft and Oracle, often for use in other corporations. Its titles will offer information relevant to a range of users of this software, including administrators, developers, architects, and end users.

Writing for Packt

We welcome all inquiries from people who are interested in authoring. Book proposals should be sent to author@packtpub.com. If your book idea is still at an early stage and you would like to discuss it first before writing a formal book proposal, contact us; one of our commissioning editors will get in touch with you.

We're not just looking for published authors; if you have strong technical skills but no writing experience, our experienced editors can help you develop a writing career, or simply get some additional reward for your expertise.

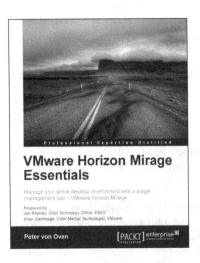

VMware Horizon Mirage Essentials

ISBN: 978-1-78217-235-2   Paperback: 166 pages

Manage your entire desktop environment with a single management tool – VMware Horizon Mirage

1. Deliver a centralized Windows image management solution for physical, virtual, and BYOD.

2. Migrate seamlessly to new versions of operating systems with minimal user downtime.

3. Easy-to-follow, step-by-step guide on how to deploy and work with the technology.

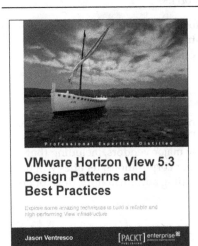

VMware Horizon View 5.3 Design Patterns and Best Practices

ISBN: 978-1-78217-154-6   Paperback: 124 pages

Explore some amazing techniques to build a reliable and high-performing View infrastructure

1. Identify the reasons why you are deploying Horizon View, a critical step to identifying your metrics for success.

2. Determine your Horizon View desktop resource requirements, and use that to size your infrastructure.

3. Recognize key design considerations that should influence your Horizon View infrastructure.

Please check **www.PacktPub.com** for information on our titles

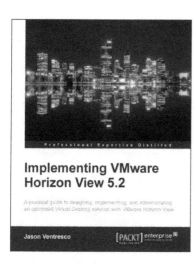

Implementing VMware Horizon View 5.2

ISBN: 978-1-84968-796-6   Paperback: 390 pages

A practical guide to designing, implementing, and administrating an optimized Virtual Desktop solution with VMware Horizon View

1. Detailed description of the deployment and administration of the VMware Horizon View suite.

2. Learn how to determine the resources your virtual desktops will require.

3. Design your desktop solution to avoid potential problems, and ensure minimal loss of time in the later stages.

VMware Workstation – No Experience Necessary

ISBN: 978-1-84968-918-2   Paperback: 136 pages

Get started with VMware Workstation to create virtual machines and a virtual testing platform

1. Create virtual machines on Linux and Windows hosts.

2. Create advanced test labs that help in getting back to any Virtual Machine state in an easy way.

3. Share virtual machines with others, no matter which virtualization solution they're using.

Please check **www.PacktPub.com** for information on our titles

www.ingramcontent.com/pod-product-compliance
Lightning Source LLC
Chambersburg PA
CBHW060144060326
40690CB00018B/3980